François Bertin

ALLIED LIBERATION VEHICLES

1944

United States
Great Britain
Canada

Photographs:
François Bertin
François Lepetit - Tanguy Le Sant

Translation: id2m

Editions Ouest-France

USA 6037764-S
19
S
C-2

American and European vehicles – very different in design and appearance.

AMERICAN VEHICLES

AN ARMADA ON WHEELS...

The story behind U.S. military power

Any army formed in America – birthplace of the modern day automotive industry – had to move on wheels. The U.S. Army was the first military organisation in the world to be fully motorised while, at the time, European armies still relied heavily on horse-drawn traction. To use some figures, an infantry division was equipped with 2,357 vehicles. The 1,038 factories - spread all over the country - contributed to the war effort and, at the end of the fighting, military vehicles produced by the United States amounted to no fewer than 3,200,436, more than 400,000 of which went to the Soviet Union.

Total production: 3,200,436
Motorcycles and light vehicles: 224,272
Light-duty, 1-ton and below (Jeep and Dodge 4x4): 988,167
Medium-duty, 1-ton (Chevrolet 4x4 and Dodge 6x6): 428,196
Light Heavy-duty 2 1/2 tons (G.M.C.): 812,262
Heavy Heavy-duty and above (Diamond T): 153,686
Semi-trailers: 59,731
Trailers: 499,827
Military tractors: 34,295
Civilian tractors: 82,099
Source: Whiting, Statistics and Summary Report of Acceptances Tank-Automotive Material 1940-45.

The major names in military vehicle production in the USA:

Allis-Chalmers, American Car and Foundry, American Locomotive, Autocar, Available, Baldwin Locomotive, Bantam, Brockway, Cadillac, Caterpillar, Chevrolet, Cleveland, Corbitt, Crosley, Diamond, Dodge, Federal, FMC, Ford, FWD, G.M.C., Hug, International, Kaiser, Kenworth, Mack, Marmon-Herrington, Pacific Car and Foundry, Packard, Plymouth, Reo, Sterling, Studebaker, Ward La France, White, Willys, etc.

USA 2187341
AMBULANCE
C 6

HELL ON WHEELS

The importance of logistics for victory

6 June 1944 to 8 May 1945 – from the Normandy beaches to the fall of Berlin and the collapse of Nazi Germany, eleven months of struggle and bloodshed were required for the Allied troops to free the Old Continent.

Today we remember the great moments of these eleven months of intensive fighting – the Battle of Normandy with its deadly hedges, the Avranches breakthrough, the Ardennes campaign, the final attack by German troops, the crossing of the Rhine, the meeting of American and Soviet troops on the Elbe River, etc. And while today we may only remember dates, we cannot ignore the incredible logistics involved in such undertakings. Hundreds of thousands of vehicles and soldiers loading, carrying and unloading millions of tons of supplies, food, equipment, fuel, ammunition and the millions of miles covered between the freed Normandy ports and the most advanced stations.

The image of America

Although the automobile came into existence in Old Europe at the end of the 19th century, it was in America that it came of age.

It was men such as Henry Ford that brought it fame while, paradoxically, making it into an everyday object – this former status symbol that became a common means of transport.

The first images etched in the memory of those who witnessed the emotional Liberation in the summer of 1944, will be of a young, sporty and relaxed army aboard a wide variety of vehicles. And while the newly arrived GIs did walk a little, their kit followed behind them in vehicles.

In their own way, reconnaissance vehicles, light- and heavy-duty vehicles, tank-transporters, tankers, bridge layers and cranes all had their part to play in the final victory.

But in recalling these fleeting images of bouncing Jeeps overflowing with crates, jerry cans, kits and beaming GIs, we must not forget the difficulties faced by the U.S. Ordnance in transporting the millions of tons of supplies – a true life line.

The further the Allied troops advanced, the harder it became to reach them with fuel, ammunition and food. This task was only made easier by the liberation of the port of Antwerp in Belgium.

A fleet of several dozen vehicles

In striking contrast with the French army of 1940, American soldiers were on wheels. And although to many, the infantry remained the "Queen of Battles", out of the whole of the U.S. Army only one in ten men were classed as infantry – so specialised were the troops.

Regardless of the weapons and units concerned, the U.S. Army had a large fleet of very different vehicles. The G.M.C., for instance, was available in 17 different models, all part of the official equipment – from standard cargo trucks to specific conversion sets and wrecker no. 7 sets.

Despite the great variety of models available, rational thinking led to similar models being built from standard modules and therefore many parts or units were fully interchangeable. Take the Jeep, for instance, which was built by two different manufacturers: Willys Overland and Ford.

This extreme standardisation meant that one vehicle could be taken apart to repair another – very common practice in the U.S. Ordnance workshops.

Light-duty

Medium-duty

Light Heavy-duty

Heavy Heavy-duty

US ARMY CLASSIFICATION

FOUR CLASSES FOR DOZENS OF MODELS

The U.S. Army vehicle fleet was divided into 4 classes: Light-duty, Medium-duty, Light Heavy-duty and Heavy Heavy-duty.

Light-duty

Includes vehicles of less than a 1/4 of a ton – motorcycles, trailers and especially reconnaissance vehicles such as the Jeep – co-built by Willys Overland and Ford – and not forgetting the Bantam and the GPA, the amphibious version of the Jeep.

Medium-duty

Includes all vehicles under 2 1/2 tons – various models of the 3/4 ton Dodge, WC 51 and 52 weapons carrier, WC 56/57 command car and WC 54 ambulance.

In the 1 1/2-ton class – 2 trucks with, on the one hand, the 6-wheeled model of the Dodge WC 62/63 and, on the other, the Chevrolet. Manufactured by a subsidiary of General Motors, the Chevrolet was available in 12 different models, from the standard cargo truck to the Signal Corps radio truck.

With the exception of the Dodge WC 62/63, all these vehicles were four-wheel drive.

Light Heavy-duty

Includes the 2 1/2-ton class and its most famous representative, the GMC.

Manufactured by another General Motors subsidiary – Yellow Truck company – the GMC was available in many models, as you will see on the pages that follow.

Heavy Heavy-duty

Includes all remaining vehicles of over 4 tons.

The 4-ton class was represented by the Diamond T truck, and the 4-5 / 5-6 ton class by White, Federal and Autocar tractors.

In the 6-ton class, other famous names could be found on the radiator grills of cargo trucks, bridge layers and tank transporters – Corbitt, Mack, White, Ward La France and Brockway. Last but not least came the "super trucks" – Kenworth, Diamond and the incredible Pacific Car and Foundry with its 1,000 cubic inch displacement engine.

1944 U.S. ARMY MARKINGS

National ID star

"JOHNNY": driver's name (not mandatory)

"LST 109": etched in chalk, indicating the number of the boat which transported the vehicle

"U.S.A": painted on windscreen indicating nationality

National flag made of paper and glued to the windscreen

"PRESTONE 44": indicating presence of anti-freeze

National ID star

Class plate (here 3-ton)

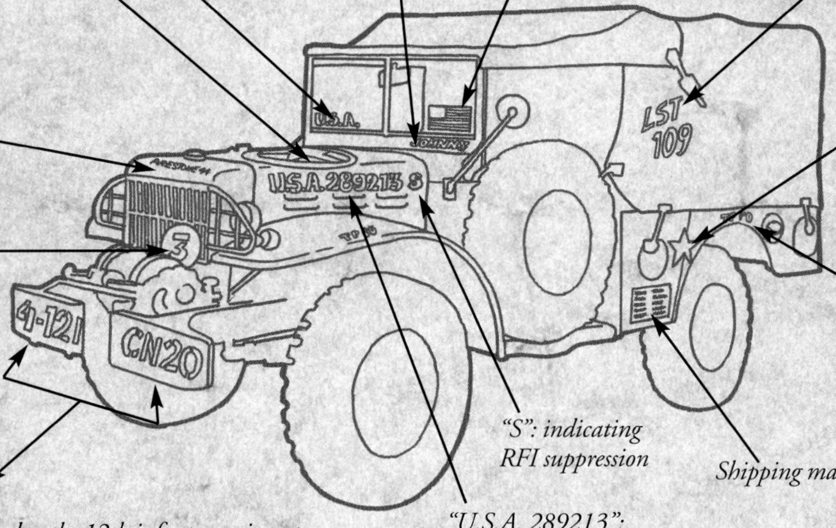

"TP40": indicating tyre pressure

"S": indicating RFI suppression

Shipping markings

"4-12-I CN-20" vehicle unit ID.
This Dodge WC 52 belonged to the 12th infantry regiment (12 I) of the 4th U.S. Infantry Division (4).
This is the 20th vehicle (20) of the Artillery Company (CN).
The U.S. Army chart tells us that this vehicle belonged to the 42nd FA Bn (Field Artillery Battalion) and that it was armed with 4-inch howitzers.

"U.S.A. 289213": U.S. Army ID number

"CAUTION LEFT HAND DRIVE": indicating that it is a left-hand drive vehicle

"MAX SPEED 30 M.P.H.": indication that the vehicle cannot exceed 30 miles per hour

"NO SIGNAL": indicating that there are no indicator lights

"KRAZY KAT": vehicle nickname (not mandatory)

National ID star

"4-12-I CN-20": vehicle unit ID

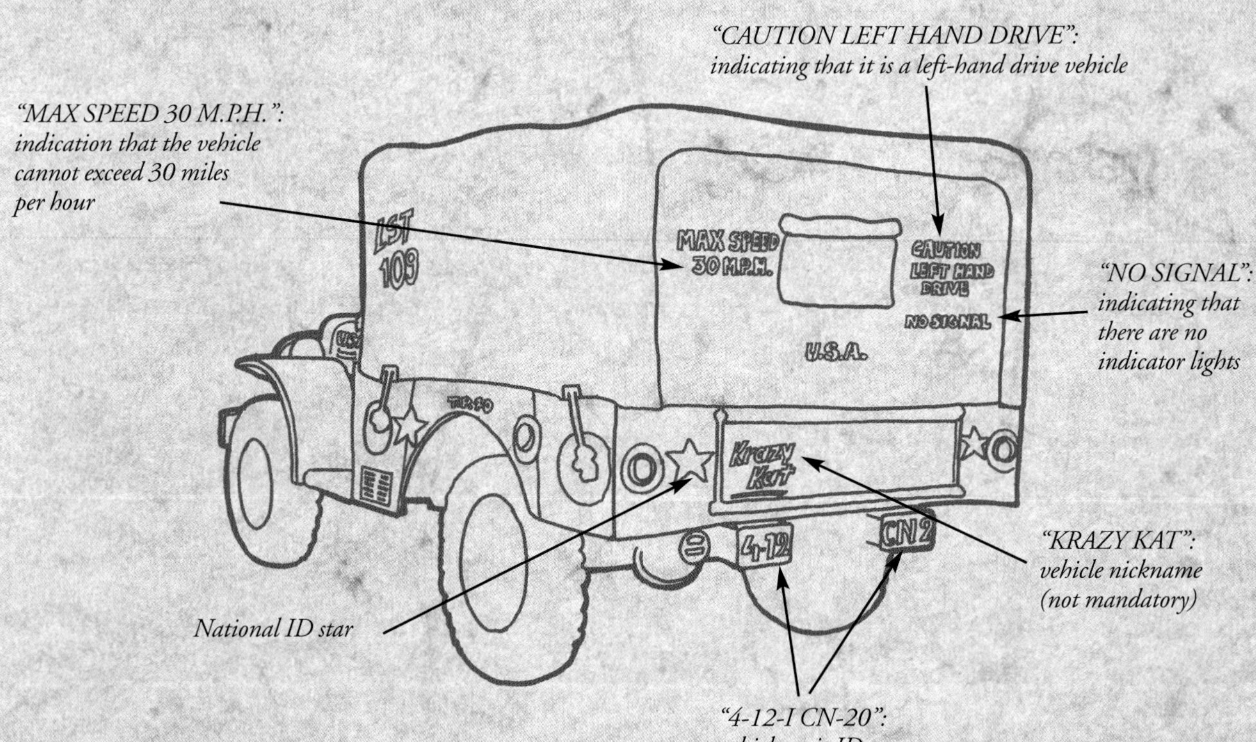

IDENTIFICATION MARKINGS

1944 AMERICAN VEHICLE MARKINGS

Nationality markings

All Allied vehicles involved in the Normandy landings bore the distinctive five-point white star emblem, which was sometimes surrounded by a broken or unbroken circle to make identification easier for allied aircraft.

Technicians from the Quartermaster Corps – responsible for all equipment – carefully calculated and studied the size and position of this star on the vehicle.

In addition, vehicles involved in the Normandy landings and the French campaign displayed a small, American 48-star flag on their windscreens.

Registration markings

The registration number was displayed on either side of the bonnet and often included the letters U.S.A. either above or before the number. This ID number was allocated to the vehicle when it left the factory and comprised a 1 or 2 digit prefix corresponding to the type of vehicle.

For instance, Jeeps had 20 as their prefix, half-tracks, 40 and ambulances, 7.

These ID numbers were sometimes preceded by the letter "W", indicating the Ministry of War, and followed by the letter "S", indicating RFI suppression.

Unit markings

Unit markings were displayed on the front and rear bumpers, and gave a very precise indication as to the position of the vehicle in the American army structure.

The letters and digits form 4 groups, which are read from left to right:

- The 1st group indicates the army, group or army corps, or else the division;
- The 2nd group indicates the unit – battalion or regiment;
- The 2 groups of letters and digits on the right indicate the number of the company and the position of the vehicle within this company.

In addition to the regular letters or symbols, such as I for Infantry or else AB for Airborne, a whole series of abbreviations was used by strategists to refer to the weapon or service, specialisation of the unit or else the operations sector concerned.

Specific markings

- Anti-freeze markings

To show that the vehicle had been regularly topped up with anti-freeze in the winter months, mechanics responsible for maintenance etched Prestone or Winterized followed by the year, on the radiator.

- Warning markings

These were added when the U.S. troops arrived in Great Britain to inform the British public of the particularities of these vehicles.

There was the marking "Caution Left Hand Drive" as well as the "No Signal" warning on models with no indicator lights.

Many other markings, relating mainly to running and maintenance, could also be found all over the vehicle, such as tyre pressure, caution when filling up with fuel, maximum speed, etc.

Other markings, Shipping Markings, which were specific to the Normandy landings, indicated the length, width, height and weight of the vehicle shipped by the U.S. Navy.

Many vehicles were also given a nickname – often connected to the name of the driver – which took pride of place on the vehicle.

Harley Davidson

Willys Jeep

Pacific M26

Diamond M20

Chevrolet

Dodge WC 54

G.M.C. DUCW

Mack 10T

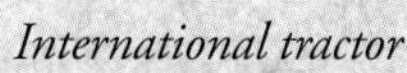

International tractor

Chevrolet

M20

Dodge WC 51

White Half-Track

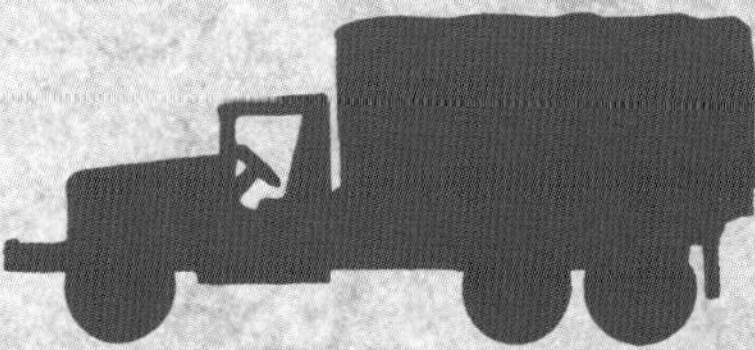

G.M.C. CCKW353

Dodge WC 56

Sherman M4

G.M.C. compressor

U.S. ARMY REGISTRATION SYSTEM

Introduced by the U.S. Army at the beginning of the 1930s, the registration system was devised to list and classify all vehicles used by the armed forces.

0 – Trailers and semi-trailers of all sizes, except field kitchens.

00 – Maintenance trucks of all sizes (lighting, small arms and light weapons), including recovery trucks.

1 – Passenger carrying vehicles (2-7 people).

10 – Field Kitchens.

2 – Light-duty vehicles (from 1/2 to 1 ton): pick-up

20 – Reconnaissance vehicles of all sizes and buses.

3 – Medium-duty vehicles (1 1/2 ton +) in 2, 4 and 6-wheel drive.

30 – Armoured tanks of all types and some special tank-based vehicles.

4 – Light Heavy-duty (2 1/2 tons) and Heavy Heavy-duty (4-5 tons) vehicles.

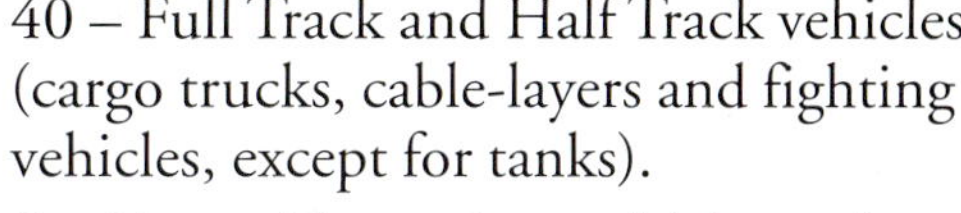

40 – Full Track and Half Track vehicles (cargo trucks, cable-layers and fighting vehicles, except for tanks).

5 – Heavy Heavy-duty vehicles and tractors of all types (5 tons and above).

50 – Fire vehicles, all sizes.

6 – Motorcycles and scooters (solo, side car, tricycle).

60 – Special vehicles (radio, office, generator, searchlight, tanker, water purifier, etc.) and armoured vehicles of all sizes.

7 – Town and country ambulances of all sizes.

70 – Amphibious vehicles.

8 – Wheeled-tractors (Light-, Medium- and Heavy-duty).

80 – Tankers and sprinkler vehicles of all sizes.

9 – Full Track and Half Track tractors (Light-, Medium- and Heavy-duty).

HARLEY DAVIDSON WLA 45

Motorcycle; Solo; Chain Drive, 45 cubic inches
(Harley Davidson, model WLA)

Characteristics

Empty weight: 536lbs
Total weight: 728lbs
Payload: 265lbs
Length: 88 inches
Width: 36 inches
Height: 41 inches
Front track width:
Rear track width:
Ground clearance:
3.9 inches
Wheelbase: 57 inches

Capacity

Fuel: 2.7 gallons
Oil: 0.9 gallons
Water:

Equipment

Electricity: 6 volts
Braking system: cable
Tyres: 4.0 x 18 (4-ply)
Armour plating: none
Weapons: none

Engine

Make: Harley Davidson
Model: W.L.A.
Displacement:
45 cubic inches
Cylinders: 2
Fuel: petrol
Horsepower: 23hp
Engine speed:
Bore: 2.8 inches
Stroke: 3.9 inches
Ignition: battery
Fuel consumption: 44mpg

Gear box

Number of gears: 3
Transfer ratio:
Axle ratio:
Gearbox ratio
1st gear:
2nd gear:
3rd gear:
4th gear:
Reverse gear:

Performance

Speed: 59mph
Ramp: 60%
Turning radius: 7ft
Tank range: 118 miles

Specific characteristics and equipment

Technical Manual

10 - 1175
10 - 1482

Note: the British imperial system of weights and measures has been used.

HARLEY DAVIDSON WLA 45

A civilian in uniform

The WLA is the military version of the Harley Davidson WLA 45, first marketed in the U.S.A in 1929.

It had a long and heavy line, encompassing the twin-cylinder, V engine; a large windscreen made from Plexiglas and khaki canvas; large, thick leather saddle bags and a scabbard of the same material attached to the front wheel fork to hold the Thompson machine-gun – the WLA Harley was definitely in keeping with the American "Queens of the Road" tradition.

23hp engine

The WLA had a 23hp, 45 cubic inch twin-cylinder V-shaped engine capable of reaching speeds of up to 62mph.

Its 2.7-gallon tank ensured a range of 118 miles and 44mpg, which was very reasonable for the time.

With a ground clearance of only 3.9 inches, the bike was unsuitable for cross-country missions and was therefore restricted to roads and tracks.

The large, comfortable beige leather saddle extends over the fuel tank with its speedometer.

A side-car could be attached to the WLA 45.

Harley Davidsons were often equipped with an ammunition or document box to the left of the front fork and a large scabbard containing the Thompson machine gun to the right. There was a siren just above the front light and a black-out headlight to the side.

The model used by the British and Canadian troops could be identified by its markings.

CUSHMAN 53 AUTOGLIDE

Scooter, airborne troops, 15 cubic inch

Characteristics

Empty weight: 256lb
Total weight:
Payload:
Length: 77 inches
Width: 23 inches
Height: 38 inches
Front track width:
Rear track width:
Ground clearance:
Wheelbase: 57 inches

Capacity

Fuel:
Oil:
Water:

Equipment

Electricity:
Braking system:
mechanical, rear wheel
Tyres: 6.0 x 16
Armour plating:
Weapons:

Engine

Make: Husky
Model: 16 M 71
Displacement:
15 cubic inches
Cylinders: 1
Fuel: petrol
Horsepower: 4, 6hp
Engine speed:
Bore:
Stroke:
Ignition:
Fuel consumption: mpg

Gear box

Number of gears: 2
Centrifugal clutch

Performance

Speed:
Ramp:
Turning radius:
Tank range:

Specific characteristics and equipment

4,734 scooters made between 1944 and 1945

Technical Manual

WILLYS OVERLAND JEEP

Truck, Command Reconnaissance, 1/4 ton, 4x4
(Ford model GPW, Willys model, MB)

Characteristics

Empty weight: 1 ton
Total weight: 1.4 tons
Payload: 1/2 ton
Length: 132 inches
Width: 62 inches
Height: 70 inches
Front track width: 49 inches
Rear track width: 49 inches
Ground clearance: 8.3 inches
Wheelbase: 80 inches

Capacity

Fuel: 13 gallons
Oil: 0.8 gallons
Water: 2.3 gallons

Equipment

Electricity: 6 volts
Braking system: hydraulic
Tyres: 6.0 x 16
Armour plating:
Weapons:

Engine

Make: Willys Overland
Model: MB
Displacement: 134 cubic inches
Cylinders: 4
Fuel: petrol
Horsepower: 60hp
Engine speed: 3,820rpm
Bore: 3 inches
Stroke: 4 inches
Ignition: battery
Fuel consumption: 21mpg

Gear box

Number of gears: 3
Transfer ratio: 1:97
Axle ratio: 4:88
Gearbox ratio
1st gear: 2:66
2nd gear: 1:56
3rd gear: 1
Reverse gear: 3:55

Performance

Speed: 65mph
Ramp: 60%
Turning radius: 17ft
Tank range: 236 miles

Specific characteristics and equipment

Identical model built by Ford (GPW)

Technical Manual

Willys
T.M.10.1206 – 10.1207
Ford
T.M.10.1348 – 10.1349

FORD GPW, WILLYS MB

THE BANTAM, WILLYS OVERLAND AND FORD JEEP

Freedom of wheels

During the summer of 1944, the Jeep became the bouncing symbol of a return to peace and freedom for millions of men and women.

Responsive, quick and over-loaded with men and equipment, it was used in arenas of operations all over the world and was both a loyal and reliable vehicle for Allied troops in the race to victory – from the beaches of Normandy to the steppes of the Urals and from the summits of Austria to the beaches of the Pacific.

This very unusual vehicle, which never seems to go out of fashion, did not arrive by chance. It was the result of draconian specifications, the expertise and imagination of a small company – American Bantam – and the efficient production lines of two big names in manufacturing.

The demands of the U.S. Army

The specifications handed over to the American manufacturers on 11 July 1940 were very demanding. The document contained the characteristics of this new tactical vehicle which would join the U.S. Army vehicle fleet. It had a wheelbase of 80 inches, a track width of 47 inches and an empty weight of 0.6 tons. It had to be 4-wheel drive and be able to carry 3 men and their kit.

2 companies – American Bantam and Willys Overland – took up the challenge. As a result there was much activity at Bantams to present the preliminary draft by 22 July 1940. Karl K. Probst achieved the unbelievable by coming up with the design of the Jeep in less than 5 days! The very first prototype rolled out of the factory on 23 September. The Bantam was an immediate success with the military authorities but there remained the problem of mass-production.

Bantam did not have the resources available for such an order and so the U.S. Army called on two big names in the automotive industry – Willys Overland and Ford.

Willys presented the Quad and Ford, the Pygmy.

3 vehicles, which were almost identical to the eye but very different in behaviour and performance, were put to the test in the mud.

In the end it was the Willys MA with its "Go Devil" 128 cubic inch engine that came top and an initial 1,500 vehicles were ordered.

After some changes, Willys factories manufactured over 360,000 MB Willys GPs and Ford, 260,000.

A forty-year success story

Easy to drive, maintain and repair, the Jeep became the all-terrain military vehicle. One of its many advantages lies in its fully standard components. With its powerful, indestructible engine, sturdy and practical design, and perfect dimensions, the Jeep became the most popular vehicle of all time.

Jeep? Did you say Jeep?

The name "Jeep", famous throughout the world, comes from the initials GP, meaning General Purpose.

Jeep was also a small animal in the Popeye cartoon, which was very popular with GIs at the time.

The Germans laid steel cables across roads at the level of the driver's head to slow down advancing Allied troops. Metal poles were attached to the front of Jeeps to cut these cables.

The basic but adequate Jeep controls. Next to the gear lever – the transfer case lever used to switch from 2- to 4-wheel drive. In front of the steering wheel – a holder for the driver's weapon.

Some Jeeps were well armed. This one features a 30-calibre machine-gun on the front wing and a 50-calibre machine-gun mounted onto a gun carriage at the rear.

The tow bar, found on some vehicles, was an ingenious invention designed to quickly join 2 or 3 Jeeps together to tow heavy loads such as items of artillery.

Whether soft-top or open-top, the Jeep really did have a very unique appearance.
The one below belonged to the 82nd Airborne Division.

The "Kübel" or German "Jeep".

Did the German army have a vehicle similar to the Jeep?

For several years, the Germans had a liaison vehicle similar to the Jeep but it was not as powerful or as easy to drive. The Kübelwagen was built by Volkswagen, based on plans by the talented engineer, Ferdinand Porsche.

Data sheet

Leichter Pkw. K1 Type 82

Empty weight: 0.7 tons
Length: 147 inches
Width: 63 inches
Height: 65 inches

Engine: 1-HQ type, 4-cylinder, 69 cubic inch displacement, air-cooled rear engine with 25hp at 3,000rpm.

52,000 vehicles of this kind were made. 14,265 Schwimmwagens – the amphibious model – were also built.

Every army on every front had a Jeep, from the United States' Navy liaison vehicle to the British troops' desert Jeep.

Nicknamed "Seep" (Sea Jeep), by the Americans, the Ford GPA was cloned by the Russian Automobile Co., as GAZ.

FORD GPA

Truck, 3/4 ton, 4x4 Amphibian

Characteristics

Empty weight: 1.6 tons
Total weight:
Payload:
Length: 182 inches
Width: 64 inches
Height: 68 inches
Front track width:
Rear track width:
Ground clearance:
Wheelbase: 84 inches

Capacity

Fuel:
Oil:
Water:

Equipment

Electricity: 6 volts
Braking system: hydraulic
Tyres: 6.0 x 16
Armour plating:
Weapons:

Engine

Make: Ford
Model: GPA - 6005
Displacement:
134 cubic inches
Cylinders: 4
Cylinder layout: inline
Fuel: petrol
Horsepower: 54hp
Engine speed:
Bore:
Stroke:
Ignition:
Fuel consumption:

Gear box

Number of gears: 3 forward and 1 reverse
Transfer case: 2-gear,
2- or 4-wheel drive.
Propeller-driven

Performance

Speed:
Ramp:
Turning radius:
Tank range:

Specific characteristics and equipment

12,700 vehicles built

DODGE WC 51/52

Weapons carrier; 3/4 ton, 4x4
(Dodge models WC 51 and 52, T 214)

Characteristics

Empty weight: 2.3 tons
Total weight: 3.3 tons
Payload: 0.7 tons
Length: 167 inches
Width: 83 inches
Height: 82 inches
Front track width: 65 inches
Rear track width: 65 inches
Ground clearance: 11 inches
Wheelbase: 98 inches

Capacity

Fuel: 25 gallons
Oil: 1 gallon
Water: 3.5 gallons

Equipment

Electricity: 6 volts
Braking system: hydraulic
Tyres: 9.0 x 16 (8-ply)
Armour plating:
Weapons:

Engine

Make: Dodge
Model: T 214
Displacement: 232 cubic inches
Cylinders: 6
Fuel: petrol
Horsepower: 92hp
Engine speed: 3,200rpm
Bore: 3.25 inches
Stroke: 4.6 inches
Ignition: battery
Fuel consumption: 10mpg

Gear box

Number of gears: 4
Transfer ratio:
Axle ratio: 5:83
Gearbox ratio
1st gear: 6:40
2nd gear: 3:09
3rd gear: 1:69
4th gear: 1
Reverse: 7:82

Performance

Speed: 53mph
Ramp: 60%
Turning radius: 22ft
Tank range: 236 miles

Specific characteristics and equipment

Towable load: 3 tons
Model without winch:
Dodge WC 51
Empty weight: 2.2 tons

Technical Manual

10 - 1530
10 – 1531

DODGE WC 51/52
WEAPONS CARRIER

The "Dodge Weapons Carrier 51" model came out at the very beginning of 1942. The same model was also available with a Braden winch, in which case it was called the WC 52. As its name suggests, this vehicle was designed to carry weapons. However, its wooden benches with folding backrests meant that it could also carry 8 infantry soldiers with full kit. The onboard crew consisted of a driver and a vehicle commander.

The WC 51-52 was powered by a T214, 232-cubic inch displacement engine with 90 horse power. The transfer case lever next to the gear lever enabled drivers to switch from rear wheel drive to 4-wheel drive. It was nicknamed "big brother" or "beep" (big jeep) by the GIs who liked the fact that it was powerful, rugged and surprisingly inconspicuous for its size.

No fewer than 255,196 WC 51 and 52 trucks were built during the war. As you will discover over the following pages, the WC 51 formed the basis of many different models – WC 56 and 57 command car, WC 54 ambulance, WC 63 6-wheel drive, communication maintenance vehicles designed for Signal Corps units, etc.

Some WC 52 trucks even featured a 1 1/2-inch, anti tank gun set on a gun carriage in the centre of the rear deck and bore the official name "gun carrier M6".

Many Dodge Weapons Carrier 51 and 52 trucks were still used by the military after the war for a wide variety of tasks. Its power and size meant that it was particularly suitable for vehicle recovery work.

Some Dodge trucks were equipped with a 50-caliber (1/2 inch) Browning machine-gun, mounted onto a gun carriage in the centre of the rear deck.

With or without winch… two different Dodge Weapons Carrier models were available – the WC 51 without winch and the WC 52 for models with a 2.2-ton Braden winch.

THE DIFFERENT DODGE MODELS

In addition to the two onboard crew members (the driver and vehicle commander) the Dodge WC 51 and 52 could carry 8 armed soldiers with full kit.

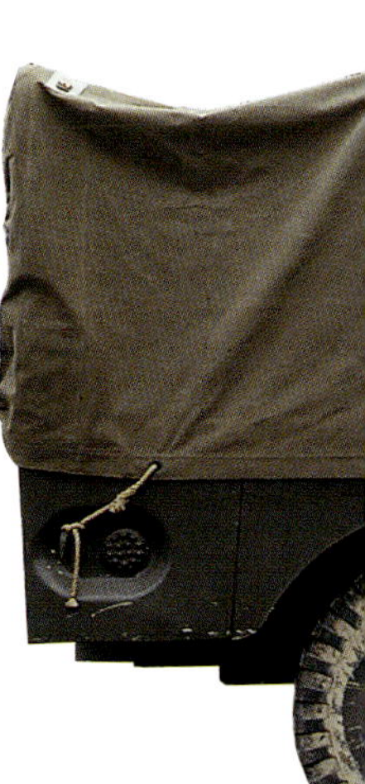

When driving down the sunken country lanes of the Normandy "bocage" area, the metal bar provided essential protection against the steel cables stretched across the road and against the enemy ready to jump out at any moment.

Some emergency Dodge trucks were fitted with a siren and a red light.

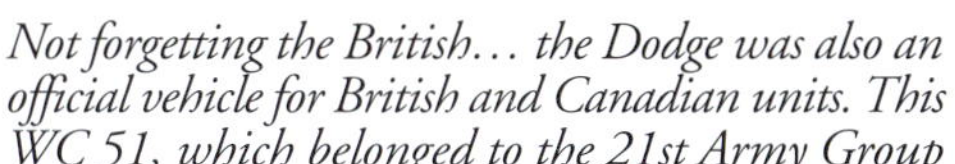

Not forgetting the British… the Dodge was also an official vehicle for British and Canadian units. This WC 51, which belonged to the 21st Army Group Headquarters, features a Bren machine-gun.

DODGE WC 54 AMBULANCE

Truck, Ambulance, 3/4 ton, 4x4
(Dodge, model WC 54, T214)

Characteristics

Empty weight: 2.6 tons
Total weight: 3.6 tons
Payload: 0.7 tons
Length: 194 inches
Width: 78 inches
Height: 91 inches
Front track width: 65 inches
Rear track width: 65 inches
Ground clearance: 11 inches
Wheelbase: 121 inches

Capacity

Fuel: 25 gallons
Oil: 1.1 gallons
Water: 1.8 gallons

Equipment

Electricity: 6 volts
Braking system: hydraulic
Tyres: 9.0 x 16 (8-ply)
Armour plating:
Weapons:

Engine

Make: Dodge
Model: T 214
Displacement: 232 cubic inches
Cylinders: 6
Fuel: petrol
Horsepower: 92hp
Engine speed: 3,200rpm
Bore: 3.25 inches
Stroke: 4.6 inches
Ignition: battery
Fuel consumption: 10mpg

Gear box

Number of gears: 4
Transfer ratio:
Axle ratio: 5:83
Gear ratio
1st: 6:40
2nd: 3:09
3rd: 1:69
4th: 1
Reverse: 7:82

Performance

Speed: 53mph
Ramp: 54%
Turning radius: 22ft
Tank range: 236 miles

Specific characteristics and equipment

The ambulance had two crew members and could also carry four litter patients or six seated patients.

Technical Manual

10 - 1530
10 - 1531

DODGE WC 54
AMBULANCE

The Dodge WC 54 ambulance succeeded the WC 27 1/2-ton model used by the U.S. Army Medical Corps.

Wider and taller with better suspension, it was powered by the engine from the WC 51 – the 0.3-gallon Dodge T214.

Its bodywork was made entirely of metal. It could either carry 4 patients on stretchers (the stretchers being secured, one above the other, to the truck sides), or 6 seated patients. The truck interior was painted white and skylights provided its ventilation. The vehicle's body was manufactured by the company Wayne, based in Indiana, Richmond, and mounted on the Dodge chassis. The shortage of strategic materials forced the Ordnance Corps to manufacture a less expensive ambulance, fitting a special wooden and metal body onto extended and reconditioned Dodge WC 62 command cars. These versions were then given the code WC 64 K.D. (Knocked-Down).

The transport capacity and level of comfort of the WC 54s were remarkable for the time. In conformity with the Geneva Convention which protected health workers, a large red cross on a white background was painted on all visible sides (including the roof) of all Medical Corps ambulances.

The British and Canadian armies used WC 54s for their emergency services. Here, the 21st group of the British army.

DODGE WC 56 COMMAND CAR

Truck, Command Reconnaissance, 3/4 ton, 4x4
(Dodge, models WC 56 and 57, T 214)

Characteristics

Empty weight: 2.4 tons
Total weight: 3 tons
Payload: 0.7 tons
Length: 176 inches
Width: 79 inches
Height: 81 inches
Front track width: 65 inches
Rear track width: 65 inches
Ground clearance: 11 inches
Wheelbase: 98 inches

Capacity

Fuel: 25 gallons
Oil: 1.1 gallons
Water: 3.5 gallons

Equipment

Electricity: 12 volts
Braking system: hydraulic
Tyres: 9.0 x 16 (8-ply)
Armour plating:
Weapons:

Engine

Make: Dodge
Model: T 214
Displacement: 232 cubic inches
Cylinders: 6
Fuel: petrol
Horsepower: 92hp
Engine speed: 3,200rpm
Bore: 3.25 inches
Stroke: 4.6 inches
Ignition: battery
Fuel consumption: 10mpg

Gear box

Number of gears: 4
Transfer ratio:
Axle ratio: 5:83
Gear ratio
1st: 6:40
2nd: 3:09
3rd: 1:69
4th: 1
Reverse: 7:82

Performance

Speed: 53mph
Ramp: 60%
Turning radius: 22ft
Tank range: 236 miles

Specific characteristics and equipment

Version with winch: Dodge WC 57
Total weight: 3.17 tons

Technical Manual

10 - 1530
10 - 1531

DODGE WC 56
COMMAND CAR

Based on the Dodge WC 51/52 chassis, the WC 56/57 command car had the same engine as the famous Chrysler T214, which had easily proved itself on the Weapons Carrier 51.

Designed for transporting officers and commanders, the WC 56 was a comfortable and convertible vehicle which could be equipped with a radio set, in which case it was coded as the WC 58. The radio's electrical power consumption increased the vehicle's voltage from 6 to 12 volts and the battery was fitted onto the step plate.

Although relatively comfortable to use, officers turned their noses up at the Dodge WC 56/57/58, preferring to use the Jeep for their operations, as it was smaller, shorter, lower and therefore far less conspicuous. The Jeep's responsiveness, agility and all-terrain behaviour further heightened this preference.

The WC 53 Carryall was more or less the closed version of the WC 56/57 command car with its special "two door, hard top estate" body.

Similarly to many U.S. Army vehicles, this WC 57 had a tool rack with spade, pick and axe for digging the vehicle out of ditches.

The 2.2-ton capacity Braden winch was extremely useful for pulling the vehicle out of ditches. This command car belonged to the 2nd Armoured Division.

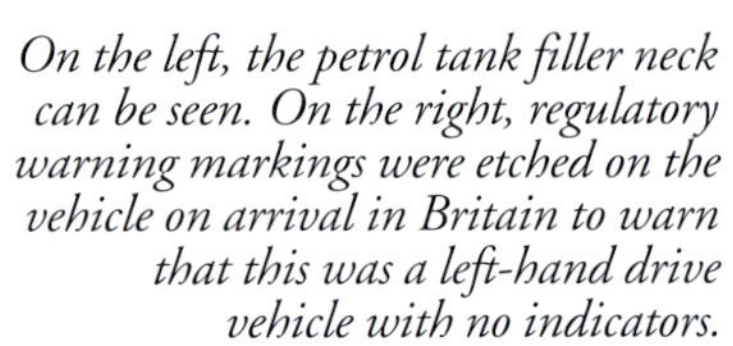

On the left, the petrol tank filler neck can be seen. On the right, regulatory warning markings were etched on the vehicle on arrival in Britain to warn that this was a left-hand drive vehicle with no indicators.

"6-WHEEL" DODGE WC 62/63

Virtually all the parts on the Dodge Weapons Carrier 63 were copied from the WC 51. This vehicle was produced as a result of an administrative ruling, which increased combat groups from 8 to 12 men. The WC 51, which was capable of transporting a whole section with weapons and full kit, was therefore given a "face-lift".

The body was extended to accommodate 4 additional GIs. Lengthening the body in this way meant doubling the rear axles and altering the T 214 engine so that it became the T 223.

43,278 WC 62s and WC 63s (model fitted with a Braden winch) were manufactured.

These vehicles were appreciated by all fighting troops due to their excellent all-terrain behaviour and solid build.

DODGE WC 62/63

Truck, Personnel and Cargo, 1 1/2 ton, 6x6, soft-top
(Dodge, models WC 62 and WC 63, T 223

Characteristics

Empty weight: 3.2 tons
Total weight: 5.2 tons
Payload: 2 tons
Length: 224 inches
Width: 76 inches
Height: 85 inches
Front track width: 65 inches
Rear track width: 65 inches
Ground clearance: 11 inches
Wheelbase: 125 inches

Capacity

Fuel: 25 gallons
Oil: 1.1 gallons
Water: 3.5 gallons

Equipment

Electricity: 6 volts
Braking system: hydraulic
Tyres: 9.0 x 16 (8-ply)
Armour plating:
Weapons:

Engine

Make: Dodge
Model: T 223
Displacement: 232 cubic inches
Cylinders: 6
Fuel: petrol
Horsepower: 92hp
Engine speed: 3,200rpm
Bore: 3.25 inches
Stroke: 4.6 inches
Ignition: battery
Fuel consumption: 10mpg

Gear box

Number of gears: 4
Transfer ratio:
Axle ratio: 5:83
Gear ratio
1st: 5:80
2nd: 3:09
3rd: 1:69
4th: 1
Reverse: 7:82

Performance

Speed: 50mph
Ramp: 60%
Turning radius: 27ft
Tank range: 211 miles

Specific characteristics and equipment

Version with winch: Dodge WC 63

Technical Manual

9 - 810A
10 - 1810A

WEASEL M.29

Carrier, cargo (M.29)

Characteristics

Empty weight: 1.8 tons
Total weight: 2.4 tons
Payload: 0.5 tons
Length: 133 inches
Width: 67 inches
Height: 71 inches
Front track width: 67 inches
Rear track width: 67 inches
Ground clearance: 11 inches
Wheelbase: 78 inches

Capacity

Fuel: 29 gallons
Oil: 1.1 gallons
Water: 2.9 gallons

Equipment

Electricity: 12 volts
Braking system: mechanical
Armour plating:
Weapons:

Engine

Make: Studebaker
Model: G170
Displacement: 171 cubic inches
Cylinders: 6
Fuel: petrol
Horsepower: 75hp
Engine speed: 3,600rpm
Bore: 3 inches
Stroke: 4 inches
Ignition: battery
Fuel consumption: 7mpg

Gear box

Number of gears: 3
Transfer ratio:
Axle ratio:
Gear ratio
1st: 2:66
2nd: 1:49
3rd: 1
4th:
Reverse: 3:55

Performance

Speed: 28mph
Ramp: 90%
Turning radius: 12ft
Tank range: 199 miles

Specific characteristics and equipment

An M.29C amphibian version also existed
25mph on land
4mph on water

Technical Manual

9 - 772
9 - 1772

DODGE WC 21/22

Truck, 1/2 ton, 4x4, soft-top
(Dodge, models WC 21 and 22, T 215)

Characteristics

Empty weight: 2 tons
Total weight: 2.7 tons
Payload:
Length: 181 inches
Width: 75 inches
Height: 88 inches
Front track width:
Rear track width:
Ground clearance:
9 inches
Wheelbase: 116 inches

Capacity

Fuel: 25 gallons
Oil:
Water:

Equipment

Electricity: 6 volts
Braking system: hydraulic
Tyres: 7.5 x 16
Armour plating:
Weapons:

Engine

Make: Dodge
Model: T 215
Displacement:
230 cubic inches
Cylinders: 6 inline
Fuel: petrol
Horsepower: 92hp
Engine speed: 3,100rpm
Bore:
Stroke:
Ignition:
Fuel consumption:

Gear box

Number of gears:
4 forward, 1 reverse
Transfer ratio:
Axle ratio:
Gear ratio:
1st:
2nd:
3rd:
4th:
Reverse:

Performance

Speed:
Ramp:
Turning radius:
Tank range:

Specific characteristics and equipment

28,537 vehicles were manufactured or almost 78,000 with the similar T 207 and T 211 models

Technical Manual

CHEVROLET G 7107

Truck, Cargo, 1 1/2 ton, 4x4, soft-top
(Chevrolet, model G 7101, 1942)

Characteristics

Empty weight: 3.4 tons
Total weight: 5 tons
Payload: 2.5 tons
Length: 224 inches
Width: 86 inches
Height: 103 inches
Front track width: 60 inches
Rear track width: 67 inches
Ground clearance: 10 inches
Wheelbase: 145 inches

Capacity

Fuel: 25 gallons
Oil: 1.1 gallons
Water: 3.5 gallons

Equipment

Electricity: 6 volts
Braking system: hydraulic
Tyres: 7.5 x 20 (8-ply)
Armour plating:
Weapons:

Engine

Make: Chevrolet
Model: BV 1001 UP
Displacement: 235 cubic inches
Cylinders: 6
Fuel: petrol
Horsepower: 83hp
Engine speed: 3,100rpm
Bore: 3.6 inches
Stroke: 3.9 inches
Ignition: battery
Fuel consumption: 6mpg

Gear box

Number of gears: 4
Transfer ratio: 1 and 1:94
Axle ratio: 6:67
Gear ratio:
1st: 47:1
2nd: 23:3
3rd: 11:04
4th: 6:67
Reverse: 46:5

Performance

Speed: 48mph
Ramp: 65%
Turning radius: 30ft
Tank range: 267 miles

Specific characteristics and equipment

Version with winch G 7117

Technical Manual

10 - 1126
10 - 1127
10 - 1438

This driver's compartment with its superb steering wheel made of varnished wood heralds one of the world's most famous military vehicles.

G.M.C. CCKW 352

Truck, Cargo, 2 1/2 ton, 6x6, soft-top with short wheelbase
(G.M.C., model CCKW 352, SWB, 1941-1943)

Characteristics

Empty weight: 4.5 tons
Total weight: 9 tons
Payload: 4.4 tons
Length: 231 inches
Width: 88 inches
Height: 110 inches
Front track width: 60 inches
Rear track width: 67 inches
Ground clearance: 10 inches
Wheelbase: 145 inches

Capacity

Fuel: 33 gallons
Oil: 2.2 gallons
Water: 4 gallons

Equipment

Electricity: 6 volts
Braking system: hydrovac
Tyres: 7.5 x 20 (8-ply)
Armour plating:
Weapons:

Engine

Make: G.M.C.
Model: 270
Displacement: 269 cubic inches
Cylinders: 6
Fuel: petrol
Horsepower: 104hp
Engine speed: 2,750rpm
Bore: 3.8 inches
Stroke: 4 inches
Ignition: battery
Fuel consumption: 7.9mpg

Gear box

Number of gears: 5
Transfer ratio: 1:16 and 2:63
Axle ratio: 6:6
Gear ratio:
1st: 6:06
2nd: 3:50
3rd: 1:80
4th: 1
5th: 0:80
Reverse: 6

Performance

Speed: 47mph
Ramp: 65%
Turning radius: 35ft
Tank range: 280 miles

Specific characteristics and equipment

Hauling load: 5 tons

Technical Manual

10 - 1146
10 - 1147
10 - 1563

G.M.C. CCKW 352

The CCKW 352 was the short wheelbase version of the G.M.C. CCKW 353 described on page 44. The main difference was a shorter rear body, the CCKW 353's wheelbase having been shortened by 164 inches to 145 inches. This short chassis G.M.C. was designed exclusively for towing artillery.

The CCKW 352's other distinguishing feature was the position of its fuel tank across the chassis behind the driver's cab. The 2 spare wheels attached to the rear wall of the driver's compartment were designed to be relocated on the front axle to increase grip in difficult terrain (see page 46).

The CCKW 352 engine was identical to that of the 353: 269-cubic inch displacement with 104hp and 2,750rpm.

Two versions of the G.M.C. CCKW 352 existed: hard-cab and soft-top, open cab.

A French version was also available: General Leclerc's 2nd Armoured Division also received a fleet of G.M.C. vehicles.

Military drivers often gave names to their vehicles and the largest amount and most varied names can be found on U.S. Army vehicles. With girlfriends' names, humorous nicknames (more or less polite), claims and catchphrases, the soldiers' ideas were extremely varied and their creations infinite. The Military police would only order the names (and the drawings that often accompanied them) to be removed, if they thought they were likely to cause offence.

KATE, LUCKY LUCY, LITTLE EVELYN, OH BOY!

G.M.C. CCKW 353

Truck, Cargo, 2 1/2 ton, 6x6
(G.M.C. model CCKW 353, LWB, 1941)

Characteristics

Empty weight: 4.5 tons
Total weight: 9 tons
Payload: 4.4 tons
Length: 255 inches
Width: 88 inches
Height: 110 inches
Front track width: 62 inches
Rear track width: 67 inches
Ground clearance: 10 inches
Wheelbase: 164 inches

Capacity

Fuel: 33 gallons
Oil: 2.2 gallon
Water: 4 gallons

Equipment

Electricity: 6 volts
Braking system: hydrovac
Tyres: 7.5 x 20 (8-ply)
Armour plating:
Weapons:

Engine

Make: G.M.C.
Model: 270
Displacement: 269 cubic inches
Cylinders: 6
Fuel: petrol
Horsepower: 104hp
Engine speed: 2,750rpm
Bore: 3.8 inches
Stroke: 4 inches
Ignition: battery
Fuel consumption: 7.5mpg

Gear box

Number of gears: 5
Transfer ratio: 1:16 and 2:63
Axle ratio: 6:6
Gear ratio:
1st: 6:06
2nd: 3:50
3rd: 1:80
4th: 1
5th: 0:80
Reverse: 6

Performance

Speed: 47mph
Ramp: 65%
Turning radius: 36ft
Tank range: 240 miles

Specific characteristics and equipment

Hauling load: 4/5 tons

Technical Manual

10 - 1146
10 - 1147
10 - 1563

G.M.C. CCKW 353

Only one figure could represent the G.M.C. CCKW. This was its total production figure which amounted to 562,750 vehicles, including both the 352 and 353 models. The G.M.C. 2 1/2 ton therefore set two records, one for production and one for vehicle life span. Many G.M.C.s are still in operation today, used either by civilian companies or by military units throughout the world.

The CCKW 353 was created at the beginning of 1941 in the Yellow Truck factory, a subsidiary and soon-to-be department of General Motors.

The CCKW 353 was based on civilian models in circulation at the time. Its shape was altered and it was made more solid to give it a less civilian appearance and facilitate maintenance.

It is surprising to learn that this vehicle was also ordered by the French army under code ACKX 353. However, the events of May-June 1940 prevented this delivery.

The first cargo CCKW 353s were equipped with a metal "Budd" type rear body. In 1943, the shortage of strategic materials forced manufacturers to create a model with a soft-top, open cab. The rear bodies were made of wood for the same reason, i.e. to save on metal.

Similarly to the 352, the CCKW 353 was powered by a General Motors 270-type engine with 269-cubic inch displacement. Its 6-inline cylinders could reach 104hp at 2,750rpm, which meant that the vehicle could achieve a top speed of 47mph.

Transmission was performed with a 5-gear Warner gearbox. The powered axles were either "Banjo" or "Split".

Many different versions were developed around the chassis of the basic CCKW 353 cargo truck, which was the most widely used model. These different versions included petrol and water tankers, dumpers, Leroi tanker carriers, pipeline layers, borer carriers and recovery vehicles.

By attaching different metal frames to the body, the vehicle could be converted into different vehicles and used for a wide range of purposes such as a radio car, a maintenance and mobile engineering workshop, a weather station, a store for the soldiers, a mobile surgery, etc.

A very distinctive feature of these trucks was the uniform radiator grills bearing the initials "G.M.C." The AFKWX 353 was a variant with a protruding cab and 7,602 vehicles of this kind were built.

What were the main differences between the G.M.C. CCKW 353 and the G.M.C. CCKW 352? Look at the body length and position of the fuel tank. The 352 is basically just the shortened version of the 353.

Double mounts for muddy terrain. The two spare wheels could be relocated to the front axle to assist movement of fully loaded trucks on muddy terrain. Chains could be mounted onto the wheels to further improve grip.

Some G.M.Cs were equipped with a circular rail to receive a 50 calibre 0.5-inch anti-aircraft machine-gun

The initials – ASCZ – to the left of the bumper on these 2 G.M.Cs above and left indicate that these vehicles belonged to the "Advance Section Communication Zone", i.e. the sector located immediately behind the combat zone.

THE U.S. ARMY'S MULTI-PURPOSE VEHICLE

A hard or soft cab?

A 12.7-calibre machine gun attached to a circular rail was used to defend the vehicle.

A trailer: the indispensable accessory.

The tractor version of the G.M.C.

The cargo version

Some recovery G.M.Cs were fitted with lifting jacks on the front of the vehicle.

G.M.C. CCKW 353 WORKSHOP VEHICLE

Truck, van, 2 1/2 ton, 6x6
(G.M.C., model CCKW 353)

Characteristics

Empty weight: 5 tons
Total weight: 7 tons
Payload: 2.2 tons
Length: 255 inches
Width: 96 inches
Height: 117 inches
Front track width: 60 inches
Rear track width: 67 inches
Ground clearance: 10 inches
Wheelbase: 142 inches

Capacity

Fuel: 33 gallons
Oil: 2.2 gallons
Water: 4 gallons

Equipment

Electricity: 6 volts
Braking system: hydrovac
Tyres: 5.5 x 16 (8-ply)
Armour plating:
Weapons:

Engine

Make: G.M.C.
Model: 270
Displacement: 269 cubic inches
Cylinders: 6
Fuel: petrol
Horsepower: 104hp
Engine speed: 2,500rpm
Bore: 3.8 inches
Stroke: 4 inches
Ignition: battery
Fuel consumption: 9mpg

Gear box

Number of gears: 5
Transfer ratio: 1:16 and 2:63
Axle ratio: 6:6
Gear ratio:
1st: 6:06
2nd: 3:50
3rd: 1:80
4th: 1
5th: 0:80
Reverse: 6

Performance

Speed: 45mph
Ramp: 65%
Turning radius: 35ft
Tank range: 240 miles

Specific characteristics and equipment

Different versions of this vehicle existed such as a Health Services workshop truck, a sewage company truck, an isothermal truck, a radio van, etc.

Technical Manual

10 - 1146
10 - 1147
10 - 1563

G.M.C. CCKW 353 WRECKER

Truck, Wrecker with winch, 2 1/2 ton, 6x6
(G.M.C., model CCKW 353)

Characteristics

Empty weight: 5 tons
Total weight: 7 tons
Payload: 2.2 tons
Length: 309 inches
Width: 87 inches
Height: 126 inches
Front track width: 60 inches
Rear track width: 67 inches
Ground clearance: 10 inches
Wheelbase: 164 inches

Capacity

Fuel: 33 gallons
Oil: 2.2 gallons
Water: 4 gallons

Equipment

Electricity: 6 volts
Braking system: hydrovac
Tyres: 7.5 x 20 (8-ply)
Armour plating:
Weapons:

Engine

Make: G.M.C.
Model: 270
Displacement: 269 cubic inches
Cylinders: 6
Fuel: petrol
Horsepower: 104hp
Engine speed: 2,500rpm
Bore: 3.8 inches
Stroke: 4 inches
Ignition: battery
Fuel consumption: 8mpg

Gear box

Number of gears: 5
Transfer ratio: 1:16 and 2:63
Axle ratio: 6:6
Gear ratio:
1st: 6:06
2nd: 3:50
3rd: 1:80
4th: 1
5th: 0:80
Reverse: 6

Performance

Speed: 45mph
Ramp: 65%
Turning radius: 35ft
Tank range: 240 miles

Specific characteristics and equipment

Wrecker device no. 7

Technical Manual

10 - 1562
10 - 1563

U.S.A
AIR CORPS
MEDICAL
SUPPLY
4208735

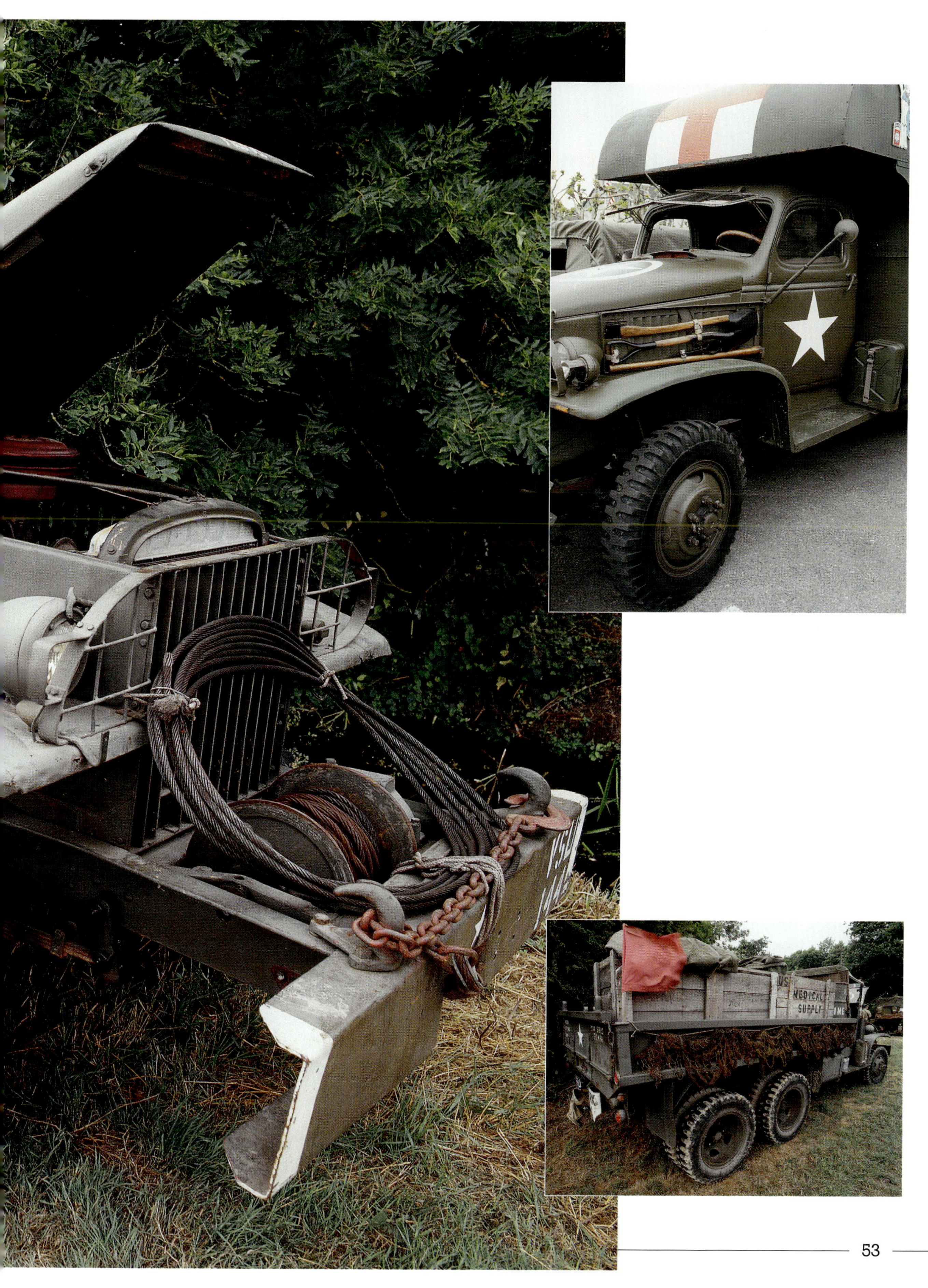
US
MEDICAL
SUPPLY

G.M.C. CCKW 353 TANKER

Truck, Gasoline tank, 2 1/2 ton, 6x6, 750 gal.
(G.M.C., model CCKW 353, 1941)

Characteristics

Empty weight: 4.6 tons
Total weight: 7 tons
Payload: 2.3 tons
Length: 257 inches
Width: 91 inches
Height: 87 inches
Front track width: 62 inches
Rear track width: 67 inches
Ground clearance: 10 inches
Wheelbase: 164 inches

Capacity

Fuel: 33 gallons
Oil: 2.2 gallons
Water: 4 gallons

Equipment

Electricity: 6 volts
Braking system: hydrovac
Tyres: 7.5 x 20 (8-ply)
Armour plating:
Weapons:

Engine

Make: G.M.C.
Model: 270
Displacement: 269 cubic inches
Cylinders: 6
Fuel: petrol
Horsepower: 104hp
Engine speed: 2,750rpm
Bore: 3.8 inches
Stroke: 4 inches
Ignition: battery
Fuel consumption: 8mpg

Gear box

Number of gears: 5
Transfer ratio: 1:16 and 2:63
Axle ratio: 6:6
Gear ratio:
1st: 6:06
2nd: 3:50
3rd: 1:80
4th: 1
5th: 0:80
Reverse: 6

Performance

Speed: 45mph
Ramp: 65%
Turning radius: 36ft
Tank range: 280 miles

Specific characteristics and equipment

Different versions: 750-gallon fuel tanker, 750-gallon oil tanker, 700-gallon water tanker and 500-gallon chemical tanker

Technical Manual

10 - 1563
10 - 1263
10 - 1269

Rear view of the Leroi compressor. Here, the French version

DIAMOND T 968

Truck, Cargo, 4 ton, 6x6, soft-top, short wheelbase
(Diamond T, model 968, 1941)

Characteristics

Empty weight: 8.2 tons
Total weight: 12 tons
Payload: 4 tons
Length: 269 inches
Width: 96 inches
Height: 118 inches
Front track width: 74 inches
Rear track width: 72 inches
Ground clearance: 11 inches
Wheelbase: 151 inches

Capacity

Fuel: 50 gallons
Oil: 3.4 gallons
Water: 10 gallons

Equipment

Electricity: 6 volts
Braking system: compressed air
Tyres: 9.0 x 16
Armour plating:
Weapons:

Engine

Make: Hercules
Model: RXC
Displacement: 525 cubic inches
Cylinders: 6
Fuel: petrol
Horsepower: 119hp
Engine speed: 2,200rpm
Bore: 4.6 inches
Stroke: 5.2 inches
Ignition: battery
Fuel consumption: 4mpg

Gear box

Number of gears: 5
Transfer ratio: 1 and 1:72
Axle ratio: 8:43
Gear ratio:
1st: 7:08
2nd: 3:82
3rd: 1:85
4th: 1
5th: 0:76
Reverse: 7:08

Performance

Speed: 40mph
Ramp: 65%
Turning radius: 33ft
Tank range: 155 miles

Specific characteristics and equipment

Front winch with 7-ton pulling capacity

Technical Manual

10 - 1516
10 - 1517
10 - 1532
10 - 1533

WHITE 666

Truck, Prime Mover and cargo, 6 ton, 6x6, soft-top

(White, model 666, 1942 - 1944)

Characteristics

Empty weight: 10 tons
Total weight: 15 tons
Payload: 5 tons
Length: 288 inches
Width: 96 inches
Height: 113 inches
Front track width: 72 inches
Rear track width: 72 inches
Ground clearance: 19 inches
Wheelbase: 185 inches

Capacity

Fuel: 64 gallons
Oil: 4.4 gallons
Water: 13 gallons

Equipment

Electricity: 6 volts
Braking system: compressed air
Tyres: 10.00 x 22
Armour plating:
Weapons:

Engine

Make: Hercules
Model: RXC
Displacement: 775 cubic inches
Cylinders: 6
Fuel: petrol
Horsepower: 150hp
Engine speed: 2,100rpm
Bore: 5.2 inches
Stroke: 6 inches
Ignition: battery
Fuel consumption: 3.4mpg

Gear box

Number of gears: 4
Transfer ratio: 1 and 2:55
Axle ratio: 7:33
Gear ratio:
1st: 47:72
2nd: 23:9
3rd: 12:9
4th: 7:33
Reverse: 53:1

Performance

Speed: 36mph
Ramp: 60%
Turning radius: 42ft
Tank range: 143 miles

Specific characteristics and equipment

Other variant: Corbitt 50. SD6

Technical Manual

10 - 1158
10 - 1159
10 - 1220
10 - 1221

AUTOCAR U 7144 T

Truck, Tractor, 4-5 ton, 4x4, protruding cab
(Autocar, model U 7144 T)

Characteristics

Empty weight: 5.4 tons
Total weight: 9 tons
Payload: 4 tons
Length: 202 inches
Width: 95 inches
Height: 108 inches
Front track width: 74 inches
Rear track width: 72 inches
Ground clearance: 11 inches
Wheelbase: 135 inches

Capacity

Fuel: 50 gallons
Oil: 3 gallons
Water: 8 gallons

Equipement

Electricity: 6 volts
Braking system: compressed air
Tyres: 9.00 x 20
Armour plating:
Weapons:

Moteur

Make: Hercules
Model: RXC
Displacement: 531 cubic inches
Cylinders: 6
Fuel: petrol
Horsepower: 131hp
Engine speed: 2,400rpm
Bore: 5 inches
Stroke: 5.2 inches
Ignition: battery
Fuel consumption: 3.8mpg

Gear box

Number of gears: 5
Transfer ratio: 1:72 and 1
Axle ratio: 8:43
Gear ratio:
1st: 7:08
2nd: 4:1
3rd: 1:85
4th: 1
5th: 0:76
Reverse: 7:08

Performances

Speed: 41mph
Ramp: 60%
Turning radius: 30ft
Tank range: 199 miles

Specific characteristics and equipment

Same model manufactured by White, type 444 T. Both models exist as a hard-top version.

T.M.

10 - 1116
10 - 1117

RED BALL EXPRESS

THE RED BALL EXPRESS: 35MPH ON AVERAGE

In August 1944, the Quarter Master Corps (the American Supply Corps) decided to build a highway – a sort of priority motorway, where trucks drove in single file at a set speed, without stopping – in order to speed up the delivery of supplies to troops at the front.

This first Highway was named the "Red Ball Express". It ran from Saint-Lô to Chartres, via Domfront and Alençon. The vehicles were unloaded at Chartres before returning empty to Saint Lô, via Nogent-le-Rotrou, Mayenne and Mortain. Similarly to the southbound route, the northbound route was also designed for one-way traffic.

As the allied troops had made sufficient progress, the Red Ball Express was extended on 10 September 1944, to deliver supplies to the 1st and 3rd Armies. Trucks then drove through Argentan and Dreux to reach Versailles where they were directed either to Soissons for the 1st army or to the East to supply General Patton's 3rd army.

As the allied army advanced during the war, other highways were also built such as the White Ball Express (which connected Le Havre to Paris), the Diamond Express, and the "A.B.C." which connected Antwerp, Brussels and Charleroi.

Goods transport

The "Quartermaster Truck Battalion", a goods transport battalion, consisted of:
1 Dodge WC 56 command car
54 Jeeps
16 Dodge Carry Alls
54 Dodge WC 51 and 52s
576 G.M.C. transport trucks
44 G.M.C. maintenance trucks
12 G.M.C. wrecker no. 7 trucks
Battalion's transport capacity:
2,000 tons of supplies

All makes and types of vehicle contributed to the success of the "Red Ball Express". Here, the tractor version of the "Stud" Studebaker US6 with a 10-ton trailer.

Fuel transport

The "Quartermaster Gasoline Supply Battalion", a fuel supply battalion, consisted of:
1 Dodge WC 56 command car
14 Jeeps
21 Dodge WC 51 and 52s
86 G.M.C. tankers
Battalion's transport capacity:
53,672.50 gallons of fuel

DIAMOND T 980/981

Truck, Prime Mover, 12 ton, 6x4, M 20, tank carrier
(Diamond T., model 980)

Characteristics

Empty weight: 12 tons
Total weight: 19 tons
Payload: 15 tons
Length: 280 inches
Width: 102 inches
Height: 100 inches
Front track width: 76 inches
Rear track width: 74 inches
Ground clearance: 11 inches
Wheelbase: 179 inches

Capacity

Fuel: 125 gallons
Oil: 5.3 gallons
Water: 13 gallons

Equipment

Electricity: 6 and 24 volts
Braking system: compressed air
Tyres: 12.00 x 20
Armour plating:
Weapons:

Engine

Make: Hercules
Model: DFXE
Displacement: 893 cubic inches
Cylinders: 6
Fuel: diesel
Horsepower: 200hp
Engine speed: 1,600rpm
Bore: 5.6 inches
Stroke: 6 inches
Ignition:
Fuel consumption: 2.3mpg

Gear box

Number of gears: 4
Transfer ratio:
Axle ratio: 11:66
Gear ratio:
1st: 5:55
2nd: 3:27
3rd: 1:76
4th: 1
Reverse: 6:58

Performance

Speed: 22mph
Ramp: 25%
Turning radius: 36ft
Tank range: 280 miles

Specific characteristics and equipment

The M 20 tractor was designed to tow the 24-wheeled, 45-ton M9 trailer.
Winch pulling capacity: 20 tons

Technical Manual

10 - 1224
10 - 1225
10 - 1254
10 - 1255

Version shown: the U6 Tractor Truck

STUDEBAKER US 6/U6/U8

Truck, 2 1/2 ton, 6x6, soft-top
(Studebaker US 6)

Characteristics
Empty weight: 10 tons
Total weight: 18.6 tons
Payload:
Length: 246 inches
Width: 88 inches
Height: 106 inches
Front track width:
Rear track width:
Ground clearance:
9.8 inches
Wheelbase: 148 inches

Capacity
Fuel: 40 gallons
Oil:
Water:

Equipment
Electricity: 6 volts
Braking system: hydraulic with compressed air booster
Tyres: 7.50 x 20

Armour plating:
Weapons:

Engine
Make: Hercules
Model: JXD
Displacement:
320 cubic inches
Cylinders: 6
Layout: inline
Fuel: petrol
Horsepower: 87hp
Engine speed: 2,600rpm
Bore:
Stroke:
Ignition:
Fuel consumption:

Gear box
Transmission: 5F, 1R
Number of gears:
Forward, Reverse
2-gear transfer case with disconnected front axle

Transfer ratio:
Axle ratio:
Gear ratio:

Performance
Speed:
Ramp:
Turning radius:
Tank range:

Specific characteristics and equipment
Dry-disc clutch
Leaf spring suspension
Inverted at rear
5-ton winch
218,863 vehicles of its kind were built

Technical Manual

MACK NR

Truck, Cargo, 10 ton, 6x4, soft-top
(Mack, model NR)

Characteristics

Empty weight: 9.3 tons
Total weight: 19 tons
Payload: 11/12 tons
Length: 280 inches
Width: 102 inches
Height: 100 inches
Front track width: 76 inches
Rear track width: 74 inches
Ground clearance: 11 inches
Wheelbase: 179 inches

Capacity

Fuel: 125 gallons
Oil: 5.3 gallons
Water: 4 gallons

Equipement

Electricity: 12 and 24 volts
Braking system: compressed air

Front tyres: 11.00 x 24
Rear tyres: 14.00 x 20
Armour plating:
Weapons:

Engine

Make: Mack
Model: ED
Displacement: 5.49 cubic inches
Cylinders: 6
Fuel: diesel
Horsepower: 131hp
Engine speed: 2,000rpm
Bore: 4.6 inches
Stroke: 4.4 inches
Ignition:
Fuel consumption: 6mpg

Gear box

Number of gears: 5
Transfer ratio: 1 and 1:38
Axle ratio: 9:02
Gear ratio:
1st: 60:8
2nd: 34:4
3rd: 17:3
4th: 9:02
5th: 0:76
Rev: 61:3

Performance

Speed: 35mph
Ramp: 32%
Turning radius: 39ft
Tank range: 746 miles

Specific characteristics and equipment

Electrical equipment: 12V for lights, 24V for the starter.
Identical construction: White 1604 with 150-hp Cummings HB 600 engine

Technical Manual

10 - 1197
10 - 1421
10 - 1545

MACK NO

Truck, Cargo, 7 1/2 ton, 6x4, soft-top
(Mack, model NO)

Characteristics

Empty weight: 13 tons
Total weight: 20.4 tons
Payload: 7.4 tons
Length: 297 inches
Width: 103 inches
Height: 124 inches
Front track width: 76 inches
Rear track width: 76 inches
Ground clearance: 10 inches
Wheelbase: 156 inches

Capacity

Fuel: 132 gallons
Oil: 4 gallons
Water: 11 gallons

Equipment

Electricity: 12 volts
Braking system: pneumatic
Tyres: 12.0 x 24
Armour plating:
Weapons:

Engine

Make: Mack
Model: EY 707
Displacement: 707 cubic inches
Cylinders: 8
Layout: inline
Fuel: petrol
Horsepower: 159hp
Engine speed: 2,100rpm
Bore: 5 inches
Stroke: 5.9 inches
Ignition: battery
Fuel consumption: 3mpg

Gear box

Number of gears: 5 forward, 1 reverse
2-gear transfer case
Transfer ratio:
Axle ratio:
Gear ratio:

Performance

Speed: 31mph
Ramp: 65%
Turning radius: 36ft
Tank range: 373 miles

Specific characteristics and equipment

2,050 vehicles of its kind were built.

Technical Manual

G.M.C. DUKW 353

Truck, Amphibian, 2 1/2 ton, 6x6
(G.M.C., model DUKW 353)

Characteristics

Empty weight: 6.5 tons
Total weight: 9.3 tons
Payload: 2.5 tons
Length: 372 inches
Width: 96 inches
Height: 106 inches
Front track width: 64 inches
Rear track width: 64 inches
Ground clearance: 19 inches
Wheelbase: 164 inches

Capacity

Fuel: 33 gallons
Oil: 2.2 gallons
Water: 4 gallons

Equipment

Electricity: 6 volts
Braking system: hydrovac
Tyres: 11.0 x 24 (10-ply)
Armour plating:
Weapons:

Engine

Make: G.M.C.
Model: 270
Displacement: 269 cubic inches
Cylinders: 6
Fuel: petrol
Horsepower: 104hp
Engine speed: 2,750rpm
Bore: 3.7 inches
Stroke: 4 inches
Ignition: battery
Fuel consumption: 7mpg

Gear box

Number of gears: 5
Transfer ratio: 1:16 and 2:68
Axle ratio: 6:6
Gear ratio:
1st: 6:06
2nd: 3:50
3rd: 1:80
4th: 1
5th: 0:80
Reverse: 6

Performance

Speed: 50mph
Ramp: 60%
Turning radius: 36ft
Tank range: 239 miles

Specific characteristics and equipment

On water:
Tank range: 50 miles
Turning radius: 18ft
Speed: 6mph
Front draft: 42 inches
Rear draft: 51 inches
Fuel consumption: 1.6mpg

Technical Manual

9802
9-1802

DIAMOND T 969A

Truck, Wrecker, 4 ton, 6x6
(Diamond T, model 969A, 1942)

Characteristics

Empty weight: 9 tons
Total weight: 9.9 tons
Payload:
Length: 292 inches
Width: 96 inches
Height: 118 inches
Front track width: 74 inches
Rear track width: 72 inches
Ground clearance: 11 inches
Wheelbase: 151 inches

Capacity

Fuel: 50 gallons
Oil: 3.3 gallons
Water: 9.7 gallons

Equipment

Electricity: 6 volts
Braking system: compressed air
Tyres: 9.0 x 20
Armour plating:
Weapons:

Engine

Make: Hercules
Model: RXC
Displacement: 525 cubic inches
Cylinders: 6
Fuel: petrol
Horsepower: 119hp
Engine speed: 2,200rpm
Bore: 4.6 inches
Stroke: 5.2 inches
Ignition: battery
Fuel consumption: 4mpg

Gear box

Number of gears: 5
Transfer ratio: 1 and 1:72
Axle ratio: 8:43
Gear ratio:
1st: 7:08
2nd: 3:82
3rd: 1:85
4th: 1
5th: 0:76
Reverse: 7:08

Performance

Speed: 65mph
Ramp: 60%
Turning radius: 36ft
Tank range: 165 miles

Specific characteristics and equipment

Holmes crane mechanism consisting of booms powered by winches.
Sliding support reinforced lifting.
Front winch lifting capacity: 7 tons.
Tanker

Technical Manual

10 - 1606
10 - 1607

WARD LA FRANCE

Truck, Heavy Wrecker, 10 ton, 6x6. M 1

(Ward La France, model 1000, series 5)

Characteristics

Empty weight: 12 tons
Total weight: 15.7 tons
Payload:
Length: 348 inches
Width: 101 inches
Height: 126 inches
Front track width: 73 inches
Rear track width: 82 inches
Ground clearance: 12 inches
Wheelbase: 181 inches

Capacity

Fuel: 82 gallons
Oil: 2 gallons
Water: 8 gallons

Equipment

Electricity: 12 volts
Braking system: compressed air (Westinghouse)
Tyres: 11.0 x 20 (12-ply)
Armour plating:
Weapons:

Engine

Make: Continental
Model: 22 R
Displacement: 500 cubic inches
Cylinders: 6
Fuel: petrol
Horsepower: 128hp
Engine speed: 2,400rpm
Bore: 4.5 inches
Stroke: 5.2 inches
Ignition: battery/magneto
Fuel consumption: 3mpg

Gear box

Number of gears: 5
Transfer ratio: 2:55
Axle ratio: 8:27
Gear ratio:
Transfer case with gear engaged
1st: 58:5
2nd: 28:9
3rd: 14:2
4th: 8:27
5th: 6:42
Reverse: 58:8

Performance

Speed: 45mph
Ramp: 60%
Turning radius: 37ft
Tank range: 199 miles

Specific characteristics and equipment

Towed load: 27 tons
Front winch: 9 tons
Rear winch: 21 tons
Identical vehicles:
Kenworth 570-573
International M 62

Technical Manual

9 - 1795 A.B.C.D.

PACIFIC CAR AND FOUNDRY M26

Truck, Tractor, 12 ton, 6x6, M 26, tank recovery
(Pacific Car and Foundry Co.)

Characteristics

Empty weight: 21.4 tons
Total weight: 46 tons
Payload: 24.6 tons
Length: 304 inches
Width: 97 inches
Height: 140 inches
Front track width: 82 inches
Rear track width: 98 inches
Ground clearance: 15 inches
Wheelbase: 172 inches

Capacity

Fuel: 99 gallons
Oil: 6.6 gallons
Water: 12 gallons

Equipment

Electricity: 12 volts
Braking system: compressed air
Tyres: 14.0 x 24
Armour plating:
Weapons:

Engine

Make: Hall-Scott
Model: 440
Displacement: 1,089 cubic inches
Cylinders: 6
Fuel: petrol
Horsepower: 270hp
Engine speed: 2,100rpm
Bore: 5.7 inches
Stroke: 7 inches
Ignition: battery
Fuel consumption: 2 to 3mpg

Gear box

Number of gears: 12 (4x3)
Transfer ratio: 1:91
Axle ratio:
Gear ratio:
1st: 5:55
2nd: -
3rd: -
4th: -
5th: -
Reverse: -

Performance

Speed: 28mph
Ramp: 30%
Turning radius: 46ft
Tank range: 264 miles

Specific characteristics and equipment

Towed load: 55 tons
The M26 tractor was designed for towing the 8-wheeled 40-ton tank recovery semi-trailer.
Front winch pulling capacity: 16 tons
Rear winch pulling capacity: 54 tons

Technical Manual

9.767
9.1767 A.B.C.

WHITE SCOUT CAR M3 A1

Car Scout, M3 A1
(White model M3 A1)

Characteristics

Empty weight: 4.5 tons
Total weight: 5.2 tons
Payload: 1.3 tons
Length: 221 inches
Width: 80 inches
Height: 83 inches
Front track width:
63 inches
Rear track width:
65 inches
Ground clearance:
16 inches
Wheelbase: 130 inches

Capacity

Fuel: 25 gallons
Oil: 1.3 gallons
Water: 4 gallons

Equipment

Electricity: 12 volts
Braking system: hydraulic
Tyres: 8.25 x 20

Engine

Make: Hercules
Model: JXD
Displacement:
317 cubic inches
Cylinders: 6
Fuel: petrol
Horsepower: 110hp
Engine speed: 2,700rpm
Bore: 4 inches
Stroke: 4.3 inches
Ignition: battery
Fuel consumption: 8mpg

Gear box

Number of gears: 4
Transfer ratio: 1:87
Axle ratio:
Gear ratio:
1st: 5
2nd: 3:07
3rd: 1:71
4th: 1
Reverse: 5:83

Performance

Speed: 55mph
Ramp: 50%
Turning radius: 29ft
Tank range: 249 miles

Specific characteristics and equipment

Armour plating:
0.5 inches
Weapons:
One 0.5-inch
machine-gun
One 0.3-inch
machine-gun

Technical Manual

9.705

WHITE SCOUT CAR M3 A1

The Scout Car had an unusual role in the U.S. army vehicle fleet.

It was created during the 1930s and showed its age in comparison with the modern Jeep and the half-track, despite the fact that the half-track was based on it. Manufactured by White in 1939, it remained the only wheeled, combat vehicle until the M8 armoured car. Its 110hp Hercules engine was rather weak for pulling its 5.6-ton body, especially as its suspension caused problems off-road. Soldiers did not appreciate its fighting compartment, which was poorly armoured and very exposed.

In addition, its size and weight made it a hybrid or a cross between the Jeep (less conspicuous) and the half-track (better armoured with tracked propulsion). 20,856 vehicles of its kind were manufactured.

The roller, mounted on the front, helped the vehicle to surmount ditches and embankments. The Scout Car's main weapon was a 50-calibre machine gun mounted on a circular rail around the edge of the fighting compartment.

The overall shape and internal layout of this vehicle clearly inspired the half-track's design.

025
D-9

The half-track.
Ready to leave for a military operation, this half-track could carry an entire fighting section, i.e. 10 armed soldiers with full kit, as well as the three on-board crew members (vehicle commander, driver and 50-calibre machine gunman responsible for defending the vehicle).

HALF-TRACK M3 A1

Carrier, Personnel, Half-track M3 A1
(White, model M3 A1)

Characteristics

Empty weight: 6.9 tons
Total weight: 8.9 tons
Payload: 2 tons
Length: 243 inches
Width: 87 inches
Height: 94 inches
Front track width:
64 inches
Rear track width:
64 inches
Ground clearance:
11 inches
Wheelbase: 135 inches

Capacity

Fuel: 2 x 50 gallons
Oil: 2.5 gallons
Water: 6 gallons

Equipment

Electricity: 12 volts
Braking system: hydrovac
Tyres + tracks
Front armour plating:
0.5 inches,
Rear armour plating:
0.25 inches

Engine

Make: White
Model: 160 AX
Displacement:
384 cubic inches
Cylinders: 6
Fuel: petrol
Horsepower: 147hp
Engine speed: 3,000rpm
Bore: 4 inches
Stroke: 5 inches
Ignition: battery
Fuel consumption: 4mpg

Gear box

Number of gears: 4
Transfer ratio:
Axle ratio: 6:80
Gear ratio:
1st: 4:92
2nd: 2:60
3rd: 1:74
4th: 1
Reverse: 4:37

Performance

Speed: 45mph
Ramp: 60%
Turning radius: 31ft
Tank range: 199 miles

Specific characteristics and equipment

Weapons:
0.5-inch machine-gun
Front winch pulling
capacity: 4.5 tons
Identical model:
Diamond International
Autocar
The M3 could carry
a section of 10 men +
3 onboard crew members.

Technical Manual

9.710 A
9.1710
9.1711

HALF-TRACK M3 A1

The half-track was the result of a series of studies carried out at the start of 1940 by the manufacturer Diamond T. To satisfy mass-production requirements the vehicle was also produced by other manufacturers, such as White and Autocar, and later also by International Harvester Co.

The half-track was powered by the 6-cylinder White engine (for models manufactured by International Harvester Co), or by a 6-cylinder 145hp-Red Diamond engine. It soon proved to be a competent troop carrier and was greatly appreciated by GIs. It resembled the White M3 A1 Scout Car in shape but with an additional half-track tractor propulsion system (i.e. suspended bogie rollers and tracks). The French engineer, Kegresse, designed the tracks, which were moulded in rubber and mounted on a metal structure. Thanks to these tracks, the half-track combined speed and agility, even off-road. The vehicle was protected by 0.25 to 0.5-inch armour plating. The half-track was the U.S. Army's veritable multi-purpose vehicle and the most widely used version was the troop carrier. No fewer than 70 other versions were also manufactured, ranging from the self-propelled 4.1-inch gun to the anti-aircraft model with four 0.5-inch Maxson electric machine-guns.

41,170 half-track vehicles were manufactured, including all the different versions.

The half-track tracks were made of articulated metal runners, countersunk into rubber, hence the vehicle's silent operation and unparalleled comfort.

Ideal for carrying troops.

Its armour plating sufficiently protected the vehicle from shrapnel or light weapon fire.

The half-track - the first American army version…

.. and the British and Canadian version

The control compartment could be entirely protected by rolling down armour-plated blinds over the windscreen and the door tops. Driving was then extremely difficult as the driver had to guide the vehicle by looking through tiny slots.

The fighting compartment could accommodate a section of 10 men relatively easily.

The M16 anti-aircraft version.
The company White manufactured the equipment and weapons on some half-tracks to improve anti-aircraft defence of convoys. These adapted vehicles were known as M16s and M16 A1s.
The weapons consisted of an electric Maxson gun carriage, loaded with four 50-calibre, 0.5-inch Browning machine guns. White built 500 models shown here, which were used by the French army, and International Harvester Co. built over 1,000 vehicles of this kind. Note the sides of the body which could be folded down so that the gun carriage could rotate through 360º.

FORD M8

Car, Armoured, Light, M8
(Ford, model M8)

Characteristics
Empty weight: 6.5 tons
Total weight: 7.2 tons
Payload: 0.89 tons
Length: 197 inches
Width: 100 inches
Height: 88 inches
Front track width: 76 inches
Rear track width: 76 inches
Ground clearance: 11 inches
Wheelbase: 103 inches

Capacity
Fuel: 45 gallons
Oil: 1.5 gallons
Water: 4.8 gallons

Equipment
Electricity: 12 volts
Braking system: hydraulic
Tyres: 9.0 x 20

Engine
Make: Hercules
Model: JXD
Displacement: 317 cubic inches
Cylinders: 6
Fuel: petrol
Horsepower: 110hp
Engine speed: 2,700rpm
Bore: 4 inches
Stroke: 4.3 inches
Ignition: battery
Fuel consumption: 6mpg

Gear box
Number of gears: 4
Transfer ratio:
Axle ratio:
Gear ratio:
1st:
2nd:
3rd:
4th:
Reverse:

Performance
Speed: 56mph
Ramp: 60%
Turning radius: 27ft
Tank range: 298 miles

Specific characteristics and equipment
Armour plating: 0.1 to 0.7 inches
Weapons: one 1.5-inch gun,
One 0.3-inch machine-gun
One 0.5-inch machine-gun

Technical Manual
9.743

In the event of an attack, the armour-plated flaps could be shut. The driver would then guide the vehicle using optical devices made of toughened glass.

The M20 version

A lighter version of the M8 armoured car also existed. This was known as the M20. The armour-plated turret armed with a 1.5-inch gun was simply replaced by an M45 circular rail mounted on poles, onto which a 0.5-inch, 50-calibre Browning machine gun was mounted. 3,791 M20 vehicles of this kind were manufactured.

Some versions of the M8 car were also equipped with a circular rail onto which a 0.5-inch machine gun was mounted on the turret roof. 12,314 M8s were built.

ALLIS CHALMERS M4

Tractor, High Speed, 18 ton, M4
(Allis Chalmers, model M4)

Characteristics
Empty weight: 14 tons
Total weight:
Payload:
Length: 203 inches
Width: 97 inches
Height: 99 inches
Front track width:
91 inches
Rear track width:
91 inches
Ground clearance:
20 inches
Wheelbase: 124 inches

Capacity
Fuel: 104 gallons
Oil: 4.2 gallons
Water: 15 gallons

Equipment
Electricity: 12 volts
Braking system:
mechanical
Tracks: 16.5 inches
Armour plating:
Weapons:

Engine
Make: Vaukesha
Model: 145 GZ
Displacement:
818 cubic inches
Cylinders: 6
Fuel: petrol
Horsepower: 190hp
Engine speed: 2,100rpm
Bore: 5.3 inches
Stroke: 6 inches
Ignition: battery
Fuel consumption: 5mpg

Gear box
Number of gears: 3
Transfer ratio:
Axle ratio:
Gear ratio:
1st: 2:16
2nd: 1:56
3rd: 0:43
4th:
Reverse:

Performance
Speed: 31mph
Ramp: 30%
Turning radius: 19ft
Tank range: 180 miles

Specific characteristics and equipment
13.5-ton winch

Technical Manual
9.776
9.1776

LES TRACTEURS CHENILLES

TRACKED TRACTORS

The American army called on civilian tracked tractors for military engineering tasks, transport missions and for towing heavy loads. These vehicles were perfectly operational and had certainly proved themselves on building sites all over the States. The best-known brand names were soon enrolled in the army and given khaki-coloured livery. Few of them were altered and those that did undergo alterations were just given additional armour plating to protect the driver in combat zones. The most widely used brand names were Chalmers, Caterpillar and International Harvester. Varying in weight from 5 to 14 tons, these vehicles were employed by all Engineer Corps units and used for a wide variety of tasks such as towing various bombs, vehicles and aircraft. With a dozer blade fitted on the front, these vehicles could be used to remove debris, clear roads and create runways for U.S. Army aircraft.

B-9

STUART M5 A1

Light Tank, M5, A1, 1.5-inch gun

(Stuart, model M5 A1)

Characteristics

Empty weight: 14.4 tons
Total weight: 15.5 tons
Payload: 0.6 tons
Length: 175 inches
Width: 89 inches
Height: 94 inches
Front track width: 86 inches
Rear track width: 86 inches
Ground clearance: 17 inches
Wheelbase: 121 inches

Capacity

Fuel: 74 gallons
Oil: 1.7 gallons
Water: 7.3 gallons

Equipment

Electricity: 12 volts
Braking system: mechanical
Tracks: 11.8 inches

Engine

Make: Cadillac
Model: 2X V8 series 42
Displacement: 2 x 348 cubic inches
Cylinders: 2 x 8
Fuel: petrol
Horsepower:
Engine speed: 3,500rpm
Bore:
Stroke:
Ignition: battery
Fuel consumption: 2mpg

Gear box

Number of gears:
Transfer ratio:
Axle ratio:
Gear ratio:
1st:
2nd:
3rd:
4th:
Reverse:

Performance

Speed: 37mph
Ramp: 60%
Turning radius: 20ft
Tank range: 180 miles

Specific characteristics and equipment

0.4 - 1.8-inch armour plating
Weapons: one 1.5-inch gun
Other manufacturer: Massey-Harris

Technical Manual

9.727 C
9.1727

STUART M5 A1
LIGHT TANK

The only Stuart remaining in Normandy can be admired at the Ouistreham Grand Bunker Museum.

During its lifetime, the Stuart underwent certain alterations such as the extension of its turret by adding a compartment at the rear, which meant that a radio could be fitted inside the vehicle.

Some alterations were made to the Stuart so that it could take part directly in landing operations and be off-loaded into water, over three feet in depth. The entire tank was rendered waterproof and an air-scoop system was fitted at the back of the engine.

Metal teeth were fitted onto the front of the Stuart tank. This device, which was used to rip away hedges, was added early on when the American troops discovered the Normandy bocage area with its hedgerows and sunken country lanes.

The M10 Tank Destroyer was armed with a 3-inch gun, carrying 54 rounds of ammunition and a 50-calibre machine gun on the turret. The British anti-tank regiments also used this vehicle, but to them it was known as "Wolverine" or "Achilles" (the version armed with a 0.7-inch Pounder gun).

DESTROYER M10

Tank, Medium, M10, 3-inch gun
(Fisher Body, model M10)

Characteristics

Empty weight: 25.4 tons
Total weight: 27 tons
Payload: 0.8 tons
Length: 235 inches
Width: 120 inches
Height: 98 inches
Front track width: 99 inches
Rear track width: 99 inches
Ground clearance: 18 inches
Wheelbase: 150 inches

Capacity

Fuel: 125 gallons
Oil: 3.3 gallons
Water: 25 gallons

Equipment

Electricity: 2 x 12 volts
Braking system: mechanical
Tracks: 16 inches

Engine

Make: General Motors
Model: 60-46-71
Displacement: 2 x 27 cubic inches
Cylinders: 2 x 6
Fuel: diesel
Horsepower: 375hp
Engine speed: 2,100rpm
Bore:
Stroke:
Ignition:
Fuel consumption: 2mpg

Gear box

Number of gears:
Transfer ratio:
Axle ratio:
Gear ratio:
1st:
2nd:
3rd:
4th:
Reverse:

Performance

Speed: 30mph
Ramp: 50%
Turning radius: 35ft
Tank range: 199 miles

Specific characteristics and equipment

0.5 - 2-inch armour plating
Weapons: one 3-inch gun, one 0.5-inch machine-gun
Other manufacturer:
Ford with engine
Ford petrol

Technical Manual

9.731
9.1731

SHERMAN M4 A1

Tank, Medium, M4 A1, 3-inch gun
(Pressed Steel Car Co, model M4 A1)

Characteristics
Empty weight: 28 tons
Total weight: 29 tons
Payload: 0.8 tons
Length: 244 inches
Width: 107 inches
Height: 110 inches
Front track width: 100 inches
Rear track width: 100 inches
Ground clearance: 17 inches
Wheelbase: 150 inches

Capacity
Fuel: 143 gallons
Oil: 7.5 gallons
Water:

Equipment
Electricity: 2 x 12 volts
Braking system: mechanical
Tracks: 16 inches

Engine
Make: Wright
Model: R 975
Displacement: 964 cubic inches
Cylinders: 9-star formation
Fuel: petrol
Horsepower: 390hp
Engine speed: 2,400rpm
Bore: 5 inches
Stroke: 5.5 inch
Ignition: 2 magnetos
Fuel consumption: 1mpg

Gear box
Number of gears: 5
Transfer ratio: 3:53 and 1
Axle ratio:
Gear ratio:
1st: 7:56
2nd: -
3rd: -
4th: 1
5th: 0:73
Reverse: -

Performance
Speed: 24mph
Ramp: 60%
Turning radius: 35ft
Tank range: 149 miles

Specific characteristics and equipment
0.5/3-inch armour plating
Weapons: one 3-inch gun, one 0.3-inch machine-gun, one 0.5-inch machine-gun
Other manufacturers:
American Locomotive
Federal Machine and Welder
Fisher Body
Pullman Standard Car
Lima Locomotive
Pacific Car and Foundry

Technical Manual
9.731A

SHERMAN M4 A1

The Sherman weapons consisted of a 3-inch M3 gun with a 2,030ft/second projectile range.

Over thirty years later, various versions were still in operation in foreign units, thus proving the excellence of this vehicle's design.

In August 1940 the American army began work on a 30-ton tank with a 3-inch, fully swivelling gun turret.

49,230 Sherman tanks were manufactured in an impressive range of versions.

The D.D. or Duplex Drive version was equipped with rubber-cushioned skirts and propellers and took part in the Landings, alongside Sherman flail tanks designed for destroying mines. With guns installed on the roof, bulldozer blades (Tankdozer version) and teeth mounted on the front to rip away the Normandy hedges, this was the U.S. army's true multi-purpose tank.

A 390hp Wright engine with 9 cylinders in a star formation, directly derived from the aircraft model, powered this hulk of over 30 tons.

Production problems led the American army to design a whole range of different engines. Firstly, the Sherman was equipped with two coupled General Motors diesel engines, then with a 500hp Ford engine with 8 cylinders mounted in a V-shape and finally even with five coupled 445hp car engines with 30 inline cylinders!

British version…

… and Canadian version

The Tankdozer

Tracks and suspension made light work of obstacles.

The Duplex Drive (dual propulsion) was a Sherman A4 which could be off-loaded at sea, reaching dry land by its own means. It was equipped with an inflatable skirt, which completely surrounded the tank, and a marine propeller system with two small propellers. Once it reached dry land, the skirt had to be lowered before the gun could be used.

The Royal Electrical and Mechanical Engineers servicemen used the Sherman BARV (Beach Armoured Recovery Vehicle) on the beaches to recover landed vehicles. To this end, a superstructure was attached to its waterproof hull which meant that it could wade through water.

British and Canadian vehicles

A.E.C., Chevrolet, Humber, Ford, etc.

British diversity and American and Canadian support

Due to the June 1940 Dunkirk disaster, a large number of British expeditionary Force vehicles were abandoned on French territory. In spite of its capacity and qualities, the United Kingdom's automobile industry struggled to make up for this loss. Canada was therefore called on for help, and the Canadians responded immediately, providing economic support and setting up an intensive manufacturing programme. The advantage of this programme, as opposed to the American one (which also helped to re-equip the British troops) was that the Canadian vehicles met British requirements in every way. Initially, the States supplied the British with vehicles that had been ordered by the French government before the invasion. Several thousand vehicles, which had been manufactured for France in the USA, were shipped to England as part of the "Lend-Lease" Act. As part of the "Reverse Lend-Lease" agreement, the British and Commonwealth industries supplied the allied forces with their own vehicles.

At the start of the war, the British automobile fleet included about 85,000 vehicles. 5 years later, the number of different vehicles used to transport His Majesty's troops to the Berlin gates had reached the spectacular amount of 1,125,000.

Austin K3

For its part, Canada produced an impressive 857,970 vehicles, including 388,299 4x2s and 50,241 tracked and wheeled armoured cars, of which there were almost 34,000 tankettes. Of the remaining 409,936 vehicles, 19,663 trailers were produced - the result of 100% Canadian technical research - and ranked under the term CMP or "Canadian Military Pattern".

Chevrolet C8

The major British military automobile manufacturing companies...

A.E.C., Albion, Austin, Bedford, Commer, Crossley, Daimler, David Brown, Dennis, ERF, Foden, Ford, Guy, Hillman, Humber, Karrier, Leyland, LMS, Militant, Morris, Nuffield, Roots, Scammell, Standard, Thornycroft, Tilling-Stevens, Vauxhall, Vickers-Armstrong, Wolseley.

...and the major Canadian ones

Chevrolet, Diamond, Dodge, Ford, FWD, GM, Montreal Locomotive Works.

Vehicles manufactured in Canada and the USA ...

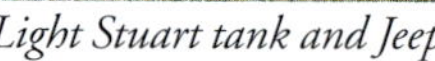
Light Stuart tank and Jeep

Dodge D15

Mack

Fordson WOT2

Chevrolet artillery ground tractor

Bedford MWD

Morris C8 GS

.... and also 100% British-built vehicles

Fordson WOT6

Morris CS8

Bren Carrier

A.E.C. Matador

A.E.C. Matador

Ford F15 and F30

Scammel Pioneer

Identifications and markings

Ford WOT2

Regulatory vehicle markings

All vehicles involved in operations to liberate France bore regulatory markings.

1 - All Allied Force vehicles, whether American, Canadian, Polish or British, bore an identical, large white star surrounded by a white (or other colour) circle. This star was painted on the bonnets and sides of vehicles.

2 - The unit marking, known as "formation cap badge", was the symbol representing the unit and this was painted on the front and back left-hand side of vehicles. This symbol was also found on the uniform sleeves and sometimes on the helmets of the men belonging to this unit.

3 - Tactical markings consisted of a coloured square with white numbers painted on the front and rear right-hand side of the vehicle. For example, a red square represented the first infantry battalion and a square with red and purple horizontal colours represented the artillery. The unit serial number indicated the formation, weapon or service that the vehicle belonged to.

4 - The registration number, made up of a series of digits preceded by a rank letter, was painted on the bonnet, front or sides of the vehicle.

5 - The class plate was a yellow disc indicating the vehicle's weight class. A vehicle towing a trailer was identified with 2 digits separated by a slash. Vehicles could drive over bridges or on roads constructed by the army which displayed either the same class number or a higher number.

License number prefixes

A: ambulance
C: motorcycle
E: earth-mover
F: armoured car
H: tractor (including recovery vehicles)
L: truck weighing more than one ton
M: light-duty vehicle
P: amphibious vehicle
S: self-propelled gun
T: tracked vehicle
V: armoured transporter
X: vehicle with trailer
Z: light-duty truck weighing less than one ton

Note: the prefix letter is preceded by a C for vehicles belonging to the Canadian army.

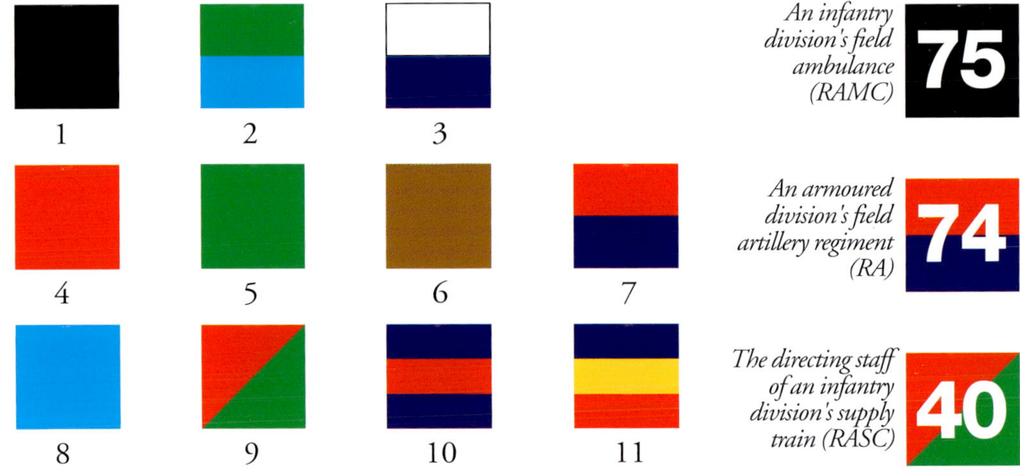

An infantry division's field ambulance (RAMC)

An armoured division's field artillery regiment (RA)

The directing staff of an infantry division's supply train (RASC)

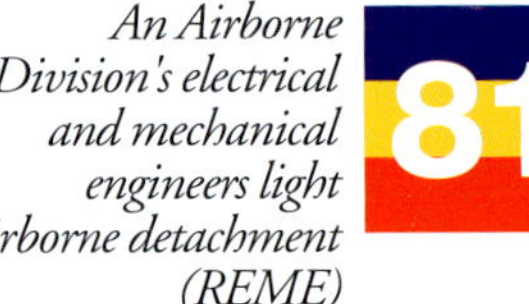

An Airborne Division's electrical and mechanical engineers light airborne detachment (REME)

Example of an armoured division's vehicle markings

Specific unit marking

Guard Armoured Division symbol

War department number. The Z indicates that this truck is classed as a "light-duty truck"

Warning: "Caution, left hand drive"

ID star

Tactical marking indicating that the vehicle belonged to the Armoured Division's Moto[r] Battalion

CAUTION
LEFT
5
54
Z 56037 S

Tactical markings

The colours used on the background of tactical marking plates indicated formations, services or weapons. In order to be perfectly legible, the unit code appeared in white on the plate. It was virtually impossible for outsiders (and therefore for the enemy) to precisely identify the unit using this number (see table opposite).

1 - Division quarter general, heavy support weapons battalion, police and military justice, ambulance companies and health section.

2 - Reconnaissance regiment (Royal Army Corps).

3 - Transmission battalion (Royal Corps of Signals).

4 - 1st infantry brigade (Senior).

5 - 2nd infantry brigade (Second).

6 - 3rd infantry brigade (Junior).

7 - Division artillery (Royal Artillery).

8 - Engineering division (Royal Engineers).

9 - Supply train (Royal Army Service Corps).

10 - Equipment and ammunition (Royal Army Ordnance Corps).

11 - Electrical and mechanical engineers (Royal Electrical and Mechanical Engineers).

A British infantry division's vehicle fleet

Motorcycles: 983
Light-duty vehicles: 495
Armoured reconnaissance vehicles: 32
Armoured cars: 31
Tracked vehicles and half-tracks: 595
3/4-ton trucks: 891
3-ton trucks: 1,056
Tractors: 205
Trailers: 226
Ambulances: 52

Each infantry division was made up of 18,347 men consisting of 870 officers and 17,477 non-commissioned officers and soldiers.

In general, a British division was organised in the same way as an American division and a brigade strongly resembled a U.S. regiment. Each infantry battalion consisted of 35 officers and 786 non-commissioned officers and soldiers.

"War Department" vehicle groups

These vehicles were divided into 3 groups according to those used by the army and the RASC (Royal Army Service Corps), those assigned to the Royal Air Force and those used by the Royal Navy.

The army vehicles were the greatest in number and the most diverse, and they were divided into 3 categories:

A-group vehicles - all combat vehicles, both wheeled and tracked including scout-cars, armoured vehicles, tracked vehicles, LVTs, tanks and their derived versions (but not including light-duty reconnaissance vehicles, American-built half-tracks or armour-plated tractors).

B-group vehicles - motorcycles, private cars (including "high utility" and light-duty reconnaissance vehicles), ambulances, amphibious vehicles (except for LVTs), all types of tractor, tank carriers, artillery tractors, recovery vehicles, self-propelled guns and trailers.

C-group vehicles - special vehicles used for engineering tasks, mobile cranes (not including those fitted on trucks), earth-movers, excavating machines, steam-rollers and industrial tractors.

The Royal Army Service Corps vehicles consisted mostly of armoured transporters but also included all the so-called "second line" vehicles, such as ambulances and fire engines.

BSA M20

Motorcycle, Solo, 500 cc

Characteristics

Empty weight: 392lbs
Total weight: lbs
Length: 86 inches
Width: 29 inches
Height: 39 inches
Wheelbase: 54 inches

Engine

Make: BSA
Model: 496
Air-cooling system
Displacement: 30 cubic inches
Cylinders: 1
Layout: road facing
Fuel: petrol
Horsepower: 12hp

Equipment

Braking system: mechanical
Tyres: 3.25 x 19
Production: 126,334

BSA, Matchless, Norton, Triumph, etc.

The motorcycle was a truly British speciality found in all British units. All the major manufacturers took part in the war effort, turning existing models into military vehicles or creating specialised bikes such as the "light weight" series for airborne troops. Out of all the makes such as Triumph, Matchless, Royal Enfield, Velocette and Ariel, BSA deserves a special mention with over 120,000 M20s and Norton is also worth noting with over 100,000 16Hs. The Canadian units were mainly kitted out with Norton 1 G-Hs (with 30 cubic inches) and Harley Davidson WLC43s - the export version of the WLA.

Carrier Tracked Universal

Characteristics

Empty weight: 3.2 tons
Total weight: 3.8 tons
Length: 144 inches
Width: 81 inches
Height: 63 inches
Ground clearance: 8 inches

Equipment

Transmission: 4F, 1R box
Clutch: dry disc
Suspension: Horstman springs
Electricity: 6 volts
Braking system: mechanical
Tracks: 9.4 inches

Engine

Make: Ford
Model: V8
Displacement: 221 cubic inches
Cylinders: 8
Layout: V-shape
Fuel: petrol
Horsepower: 60hp at 2,840rpm
Fuel tank: 20 gallons

Tankettes

A 100% British product… The manufacturers – Carden-Loyd and Vickers-Armstrong – developed the principle behind the tankette during the inter-war years. This small, full-track vehicle was widely used by British armies and throughout the entire Commonwealth. Originally designed for reconnaissance missions, different versions of the tankette were developed based on the original body. The vehicle was used to transport a wide variety of ammunition and equipment and also personnel, and versions also existed with a mine thrower and a light gun. The most common versions featured a Bren machine-gun on the front. Although different manufacturers such as Ford, Thornycroft, Wolseley, Dennis, Sentinel, etc., built the vehicle itself, all tankettes were powered by the 221-cubic inch Ford V8 engine which was fitted at the rear.

Bren Carrier

Windsor Mk1

T28793

The tankette - an essentially British concept

Humber FWD

Car, Heavy Utility, 4x4, Humber

Characteristics

Empty weight: 2.1 tons
Total weight: 2.7 tons
Length: 168 inches
Width: 77 inches
Height: 81 inches
Ground clearance: 9 inches
Wheelbase: 112 inches

Engine

Make: Humber
Model: 6
Water-cooling system
Displacement: 249 cubic inches
Cylinders: 6
Layout: inline
Fuel: petrol
Horsepower: 85hp at 3,400rpm
Fuel tank: 16 gallons

Equipment

Transmission: 4 gears
4-wheel drive
Transfer case: 2-gear with disconnected front axlc
Clutch: dry disc
Independent front-wheel suspension with transverse springs
Rear suspension with solid axles suspended by leaf springs
Electricity: 6 volts
Braking system: hydraulic
Tyres: 9.25 x 16
Use: liaison and command vehicle

Liaison and command vehicles

For their liaison vehicles, the British used many civilian models which they converted for military use and gave specific markings. They also created a fleet of vehicles with carrying and passability capacities that were more suitable for field use. The most common models were the Humber FWD 4x4 Heavy Utility and the Ford WOA 2A 2-wheel drive, which were used as liaison and command vehicles. The Canadians preferred the Chevrolet Heavy Utility with its characteristic front.

And last but not least, the Jeep which was used by all units. The one shown here was used by the airborne troops. These vehicles often underwent conversion work according to particular requirements. For example, the grill and bumper were removed and armour plating and additional equipment were attached.

Daimler MKII Dingo

Car Scout, 4x4, Daimler

Characteristics

Empty weight: 2.6 tons
Total weight: 2.9 tons
Length: 125 inches
Width: 67 inches
Height: 59 inches
Wheelbase: 78 inches

Engine

Make: Daimler
Model: 18 HP
Overhead valves
Displacement: 154 cubic inches
Cylinders: 6
Layout: inline
Fuel: petrol
Horsepower: 55hp
Tank range: 199 miles
Speed: 53mph

Equipment

Transmission: preselector 5-gear box
Permanent 4-wheel drive
Transfer case: single speed with reversing gear
Clutch: dry disc
Spring suspension
Wheels suspended independently
Electricity: 12 volts
Braking system: hydraulic
Tyres: 7.0 x 18
Production: 6,626 vehicles
Crew: 2
Weapons: 1 Bren machine-gun
Armour plating: 1.2 inches
Use: reconnaissance and liaison

Humber MK1

Car Scout, 4x4, Humber

Characteristics

Total weight: 3.8 tons
Length: 151 inches
Width: 74 inches
Height: 84 inches
Wheelbase: 91 inches

Engine

Make: Roots
Model: 4088
Displacement: 249 cubic inches
Cylinders: 6
Layout: inline
Fuel: petrol
Horsepower: 87hp
Tank range: 199 miles
Speed: 56mph

Equipment

Transmission: 4-gear box
2- or 4-wheel drive
Clutch: dry disc
Spring-leaf suspension
Transverse springs at front
Electricity: 12 volts
Braking system: hydraulic
Tyres: 9.25 x 16
Production: 4,300 vehicles
Crew: 3
Weapons: 1 or 2 Bren machine-guns
Armour plating: 0.6 inches
Use: reconnaissance and liaison

Bedford MWD

Truck, 15 cwt, GS, 4x2, Bedford

Characteristics

Empty weight: 2.1 tons
Total weight: 3.5 tons
Length: 172 inches
Width: 78 inches
Height: 90 inches
Ground clearance: 9 inches
Wheelbase: 99 inches

Engine

Make: Bedford
Model: 6
Overhead valves
Water-cooling system
Displacement: 215 cubic inches
Cylinders: 6
Layout: inline
Fuel: petrol
Horsepower: 72hp at 3,000rpm
Fuel tank: 20 gallons

Equipment

Transmission: 4-gear box
2-wheel drive
Clutch: dry disc
Suspension: solid axles suspended by semi-elliptic springs
Electricity: 12 volts
Braking system: hydraulic
Tyres: 9.0 x 16
Production: 66,000 vehicles

F 60L AMB à caisse Lindsay

Ford C 298 QF-F 60L

Truck, 3 ton, GS, 4x4, Ford

Characteristics

Empty weight: 4.3 tons
Total weight: 7.1 tons
Length: 244 inches
Width: 90 inches
Height: 75 inches
Ground clearance: 11 inches
Wheelbase: 158 inches

Engine

Make: Ford
Model: 239 V8
Side valves
Water-cooling system
Displacement: 239 cubic inches
Cylinders: 8
Layout: V-shape
Fuel: petrol
Horsepower: 95hp at 3,600rpm
Fuel tank: 25 gallons

Equipment

Transmission: 4-gear box
4-wheel drive
Transfer case: 2-gear with disconnected front axle
Clutch: dry disc
Suspension: solid axles suspended by semi-elliptic springs
Electricity: 6 volts
Braking system: hydraulic with servo assist
Tyres: 10.5 x 20
Production: 209,000 vehicles

Ford WOT 2

Truck, 15 cwt, 4x2, Ford

Characteristics

Empty weight: 2.0 tons
Total weight: 3.3 tons
Length: 177 inches
Width: 79 inches
Height: 90 inches
(minimum: 71 inches)
Ground clearance: 11 inches
Wheelbase: 106 inches

Engine

Make: Ford
Model: 30 HP V8
Displacement: 221 cubic inches
Cylinders: 8
Layout: V-shape
Fuel: petrol
Horsepower: 60hp at 2,840rpm
Fuel tank: 23 gallons

Equipment

Transmission: 4-gear box
2-wheel drive
Clutch: dry disc
Suspension: solid axles suspended
by semi-elliptic springs
(transverse springs at front)
Electricity: 12 volts
Braking system: mechanical
Tyres: 9.0 x 16
Production: 60,000 vehicles

C8A HUP

Chevrolet 8445-C8 A

Truck, Heavy Utility, Personnel, 4x4, Chevrolet

Characteristics

Empty weight: 2.8 tons
Total weight: 3.3 tons
Length: 163 inches
Width: 79 inches
Height: 90 inches
Ground clearance: 9 inches
Wheelbase: 101 inches

Engine

Make: Chevrolet
Model: 216
Overhead valves
Displacement: 221 cubic inches
Cylinders: 6
Layout: inline
Fuel: petrol
Horsepower: 85hp at 3,400rpm
Fuel tank: 25 gallons

Equipment

Transmission: 4-gear box
4-wheel drive
Transfer case: single speed, disconnected front axle
Clutch: dry disc
Suspension: solid axles suspended by semi-elliptic springs
Electricity: 6 volts
Braking system: hydraulic
Tyres: 9.25 x 16
Production: 13,000 vehicles

C8A HUW radio

Morris Commercial CS 8

Truck, 15 cwt, 4x2, Morris Commercial

Characteristics

Empty weight: 2 tons
Total weight: 3 tons
Length: 166 inches
Width: 78 inches
Height: 89 inches
(66 inches minimum)
Ground clearance: 5 inches
Wheelbase: 98 inches

Engine

Make: Morris
Model: OH
Side valves
Water-cooling system
Displacement: 213 cubic inches
Cylinders: 6
Layout: inline
Fuel: petrol
Horsepower: 60hp at 2,800rpm
Fuel tank: 22 gallons

Equipment

Transmission: 4-gear box
2-wheel drive
Clutch: dry disc
Suspension: solid axles suspended by semi-elliptic springs
Electricity: 12 volts
Braking system: mechanical
Tyres: 9.0 x 16

C8 MKII artillery tractor

Morris Commercial

Morris Commercial built a wide range of all types of military vehicles designed for the most diverse uses. Its most common vehicle was the CS8.

The C8 AT was an artillery tractor which was modified so that it could carry an anti-tank gun.

A unique front

The "Self Propelled Bofors Vehicle" was the result of mounting a 1.6-inch Bofors anti-aircraft gun onto a Morris C9B chassis. This vehicle was used by the Royal Artillery light Anti-aircraft Regiments. A version mounted on a 3-ton Ford truck chassis also existed for Canada.

Chevrolet Canada 8421-C15

Truck, 15 cwt, GS, 4x4, Ford

Characteristics

Empty weight: 3 tons
Total weight: 3.8 tons
Length: 170 inches
Width: 87 inches
Height: 86 inches
Ground clearance: 8 inches
Wheelbase: 101 inches

Engine

Make: Chevrolet
Model: 216
Displacement: 216 cubic inches
Cylinders: 6
Layout: inline
Fuel: petrol
Horsepower: 85hp at 3,100rpm
Fuel tank: 25 gallons

Equipment

Transmission: 4-gear box
2- or 4-wheel drive
Transfer case: single speed and disconnected front axle on the 4x4 version
Clutch: dry disc
Suspension: solid axles suspended by semi-elliptic springs
Electricity: 6 volts
Braking system: hydraulic
Tyres: 9.0 x 16
Used in conjunction with the Ford F15A

Bedford QLD

Truck, 3 ton, 4x4, Bedford

Characteristics

Empty weight: 3.2 tons
Total weight: 6.9 tons
Length: 236 inches
Width: 89 inches
Height: 120 inches
(102 inches minimum)
Ground clearance: 12 inches
Wheelbase: 143 inches

Engine

Make: Bedford
Model: 6
Displacement: 215 cubic inches
Cylinders: 6
Layout: inline
Fuel: petrol
Horsepower: 72hp at 3,000rpm
Fuel tank: 28 gallons

Equipment

Transmission: 4-gear box
4-wheel drive
Clutch: dry disc
Suspension: solid axles suspended by semi-elliptic springs
Electricity: 12 volts
Braking system: hydraulic with servo assist
Tyres: 10.5 x 20
Production: 52,250 vehicles

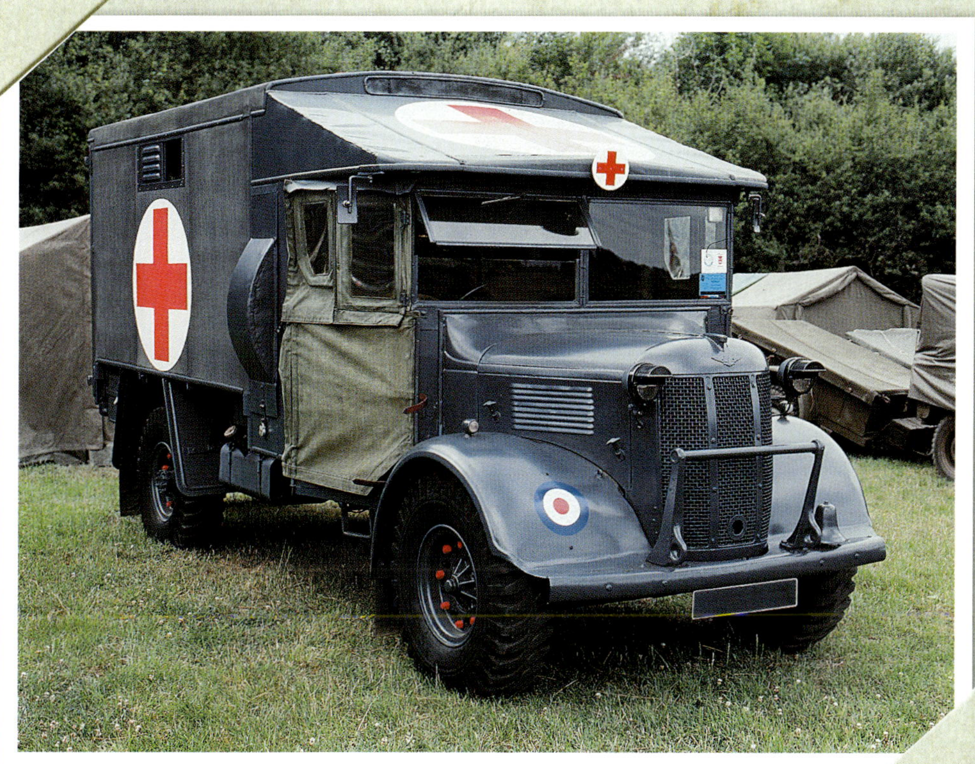

Austin K2-Y

Truck, 2 ton, 4x2, Ambulance, Austin

Characteristics

Empty weight: 3.1 tons
Length: 216 inches
Width: 87 inches
Height: 110 inches
Ground clearance: inches
Wheelbase: 134 inches

Engine

Make: Austin
Model: 6
Overhead valves
Displacement: 211 cubic inches
Cylinders: 6
Layout: inline
Fuel: petrol
Horsepower: 63hp

Equipment

Transmission: 4-gear box
2-wheel drive
Clutch: dry disc
Suspension: leaf spring
4 stretchers or 10 seated patients
Braking system: hydraulic
Tyres: 10.5 x 16
Production: 13,000 vehicles

AEC Matador

Tractor, 4x4, Medium Artillery, AEC

Characteristics

Empty weight: 7.1 tons
Total weight: 11.3 tons
Length: 249 inches
Width: 94 inches
Height: 122 inches
Ground clearance: inches
Wheelbase: 152 inches

Engine

Make: AEC
Model: A 173
Displacement: 463 cubic inches
Cylinders: 6
Layout: inline
Fuel: diesel
Horsepower: 95hp
Fuel tank: 40 gallons

Equipment

Transmission: 4-gear box
2- or 4-wheel drive
Clutch: dry disc
Suspension: leaf spring
Braking system: hydraulic with servo assist
Tyres: 13.5 x 20
Production: 10,000 vehicles

Leyland Hippo MK2

Truck, 10 ton, 6x4, GS, Leyland

Characteristics

Empty weight: 9.4 tons
Length: 327 inches
Width: 97 inches
Height: 131 inches
Wheelbase: 186 inches

Engine

Make: Leyland
Model: L
Displacement: 452 cubic inches
Cylinders: 6
Layout: inline
Fuel: diesel
Horsepower: 100hp

Equipment

Transmission: 5-gear box
4-wheel drive, 6x4
Auxiliary drive: 2-gear
Clutch: dry disc
Suspension: leaf spring reversed at rear
Braking system: hydraulic with servo assist
Tyres: 13.5 x 20

Scammel Pioneer R100

Recovery Truck, 6x4, Scammel

Characteristics

Empty weight: 8.4 tons
Length: 247 inches
Width: 102 inches
Height: 117 inches
Wheelbase: 146 inches

Engine

Make: Gardner
Model: 6 LW
Displacement: 511 cubic inches
Cylinders: 6
Layout: inline
Fuel: diesel
Horsepower: 102hp
Fuel tank: 54 gallons

Equipment

Transmission: 6-gear box
Clutch: dry disc
Suspension: transverse leaf springs at front
Braking system: mechanical with servo assist
Tyres: 13.5 x 20
Production: 768 vehicles

British and Canadian tanks

For light-duty tanks, the British army used the American Stuart M3 A3 which they renamed "Honey". This tank weighed 13 tons and was armed with a 1.5-inch gun.

For medium-duty tanks, the British used the 100%-British manufactured, 28-ton Cromwell IV with its 3-inch gun, of which many different versions existed and which was used for reconnaissance and combat missions. They also used the 30-ton Centaur IV inspired by the Cromwell but armed with a 4-inch howitzer and used as an infantry support tank. The "Challenger" was another British vehicle, with a 17-pounder gun mounted on a Cromwell chassis.

For heavy-duty tanks for infantry support missions, the British used the "Churchill". This weighed 40 tons and was armed with just one 6-pounder gun, later replaced, as the fighting progressed, by a 3-inch gun. Its body was used as a basis for various versions, of which the most famous were the "Hobarth's Funnies" – special tanks which took part in the Landings with the first line of assault.

The USA manufactured the vast majority of equipment for the British Armoured Regiments including the Sherman M4, armed with a 3-inch gun. To strike back against the 3.5-inch German guns, the "Firefly" version was fitted with the powerful British 17-pounder (3-inch) gun for superior performance.

All in all, 17,165 Sherman M4 tanks were manufactured for the British army.

For its anti-tank missions, the British used the American M10 Destroyer tank known as "Wolverine". The self-propelled artillery was equipped with the American "Priest" self-propelled gun, armed with a 4-inch howitzer and the "Sexton". The Sexton, which looked like the M7, was built in Canada and was armed with a 25-pounder (3.5-inch) gun.

The American-built Sherman M4 Medium Tank was the only vehicle used by the Canadian Armoured Regiments as a combat tank. The reconnaissance units used light-duty Stuart M3 A3s and, similarly to their British counterparts, the self-propelled artillery used Centaur IVs, M7 Priests and Sextons.

The "Sexton", with a gun mounted on a Canadian Ram chassis, was used by both the British and Canadian armoured units.

Cromwell Leyland A27M

Tank, Cruiser Mk VIII, Cromwell

Characteristics

Empty weight: 26.3 tons
Total weight: 27.7 tons
Length: 250 inches
Width: 114 inches
Height: 99 inches

Engine

Make: Rolls-Royce
Model: Meteor
Displacement: 1,649 cubic inches
Cylinders: 12
Layout: V-shape
Fuel: diesel
Horsepower: 600hp

Equipment

Transmission:
Merritt-Brown 5-gear box
Suspension: Christie
Electricity: volts
Braking system: hydraulic
Tracks: 14 and 15 inches
Max. speed: 40mph
Armour plating: 0.8/3 inches
Crew: 5

Churchill MK IV

Tank, Infantry, MK IV, Vauxhall A22

Characteristics

Empty weight: 41 tons
Length: 302 inches
Width: 128 inches
Height: 98 inches
Ground clearance: 20 inches

Engine

Make: Vauxhall
Model: Twin-Six HQ
Side valves
Displacement: 1,296 cubic inches
Cylinders: 12
Layout: two banks of inline cylinders
Fuel: petrol
Horsepower: 350hp at 2,200rpm
Fuel tank: 148 gallons

Equipment

Transmission: Merritt-Brown 4-gear box
Clutch: dry disc
Suspension: bogies and springs (2 x 11)
Electricity: 12 volts
Tracks: 14 inches
Production: 5,640 vehicles

40

By way of conclusion

Choosing which American, Canadian and British vehicles to include in this book was a difficult task. Some may feel that certain vehicles are missing, however the main purpose of this book was to give a concise overview of Allied military vehicles. Several hundred pages would have been necessary if the aim of the book had been to compose an exhaustive catalogue of all vehicles used by the allied armies in the liberation of Europe.

May those who are passionate about such vehicles forgive me.

I would like to thank all those who so kindly lent their support during the creation of this book, including collectors, restorer-technicians and military specialists.

Many thanks also to Philippe Lambard for so kindly sharing his knowledge with me and for his warm support.

I am particularly grateful to Tanguy Le Sant and François Lepetit who often went to great lengths to help me with my research and who also added to my photo collection, donating rare items from their personal collections.

Without their help and enthusiasm this book would not have been possible.

François Bertin

USAF
00 95748
The
BLONDE
BOMBSHELL

Table of contents

Editor : Servane Biguais
Layout : Ad Lib, Rennes
Photoengraving : Scann'Ouest, Rennes
Printing : Imprimerie Pollina, à Luçon (85) - n° L45310A

I.S.B.N. 978.2.7373.3465.8 - Publisher n° : 4702.04.1,5.03.08
Legal deposit : February 2004 - Printed in France.
www.editionsouestfrance.fr